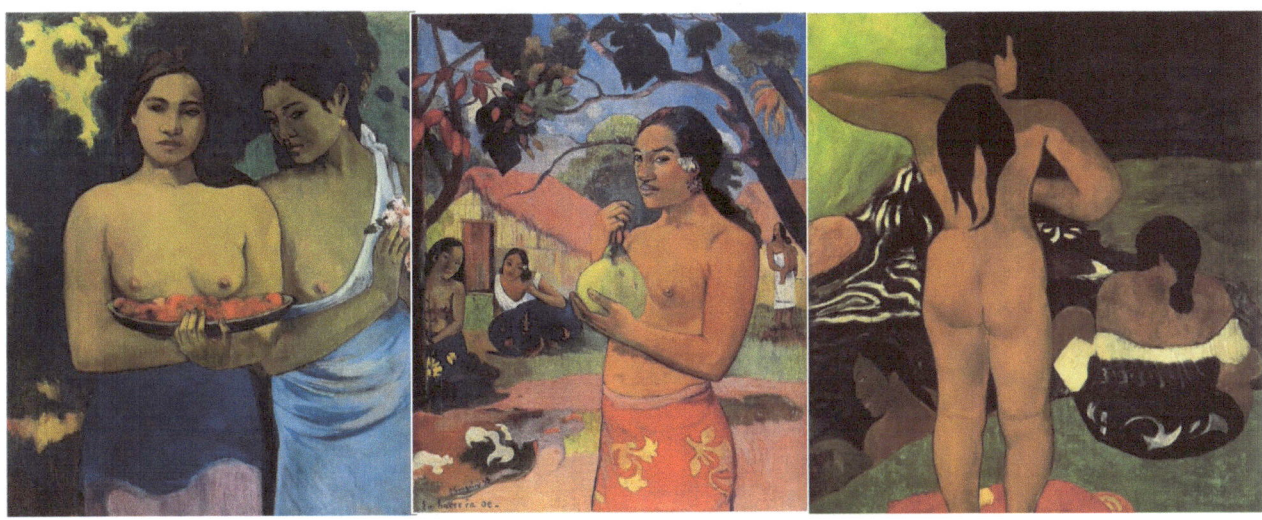

Paul Gauguin

Edited by Lacey Belinda Smith

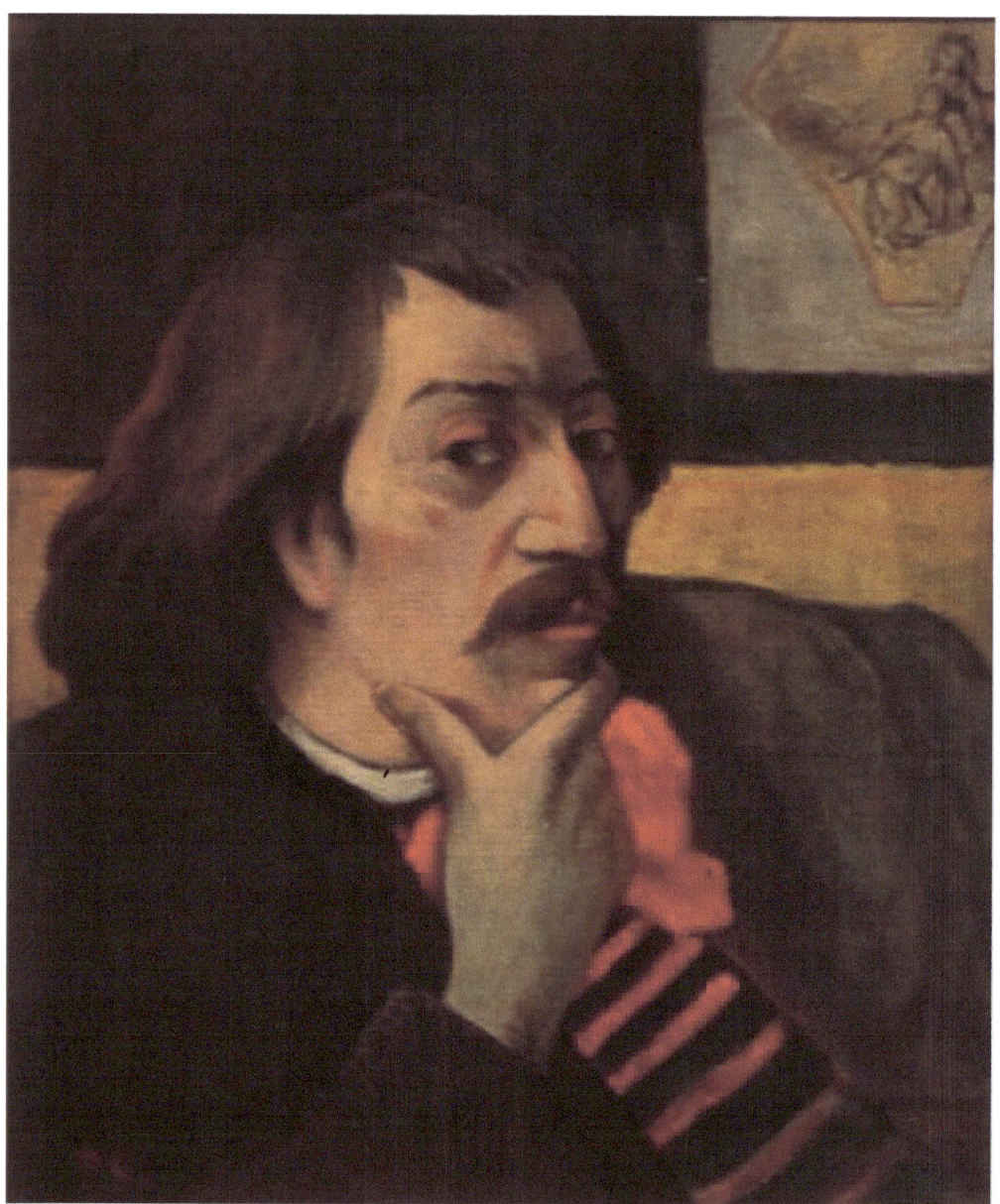

Paul Gauguin--Self-Portrait 1893

Eugène Henri Paul Gauguin (1848 – 1903) was a leading French Post-Impressionist artist.

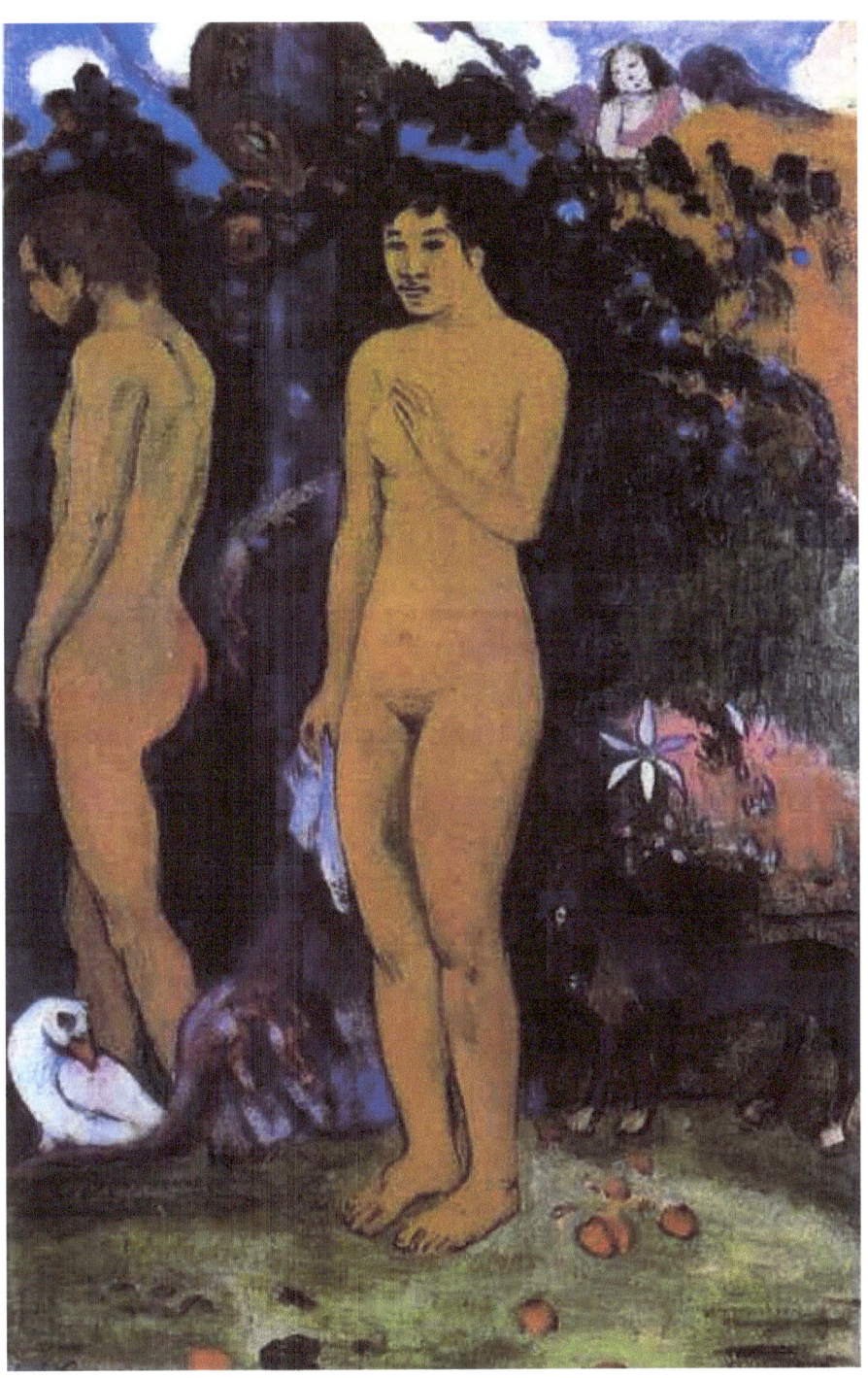

Adam and Eve—1902--French Polynesia--Post-Impressionism--2nd Tahiti period

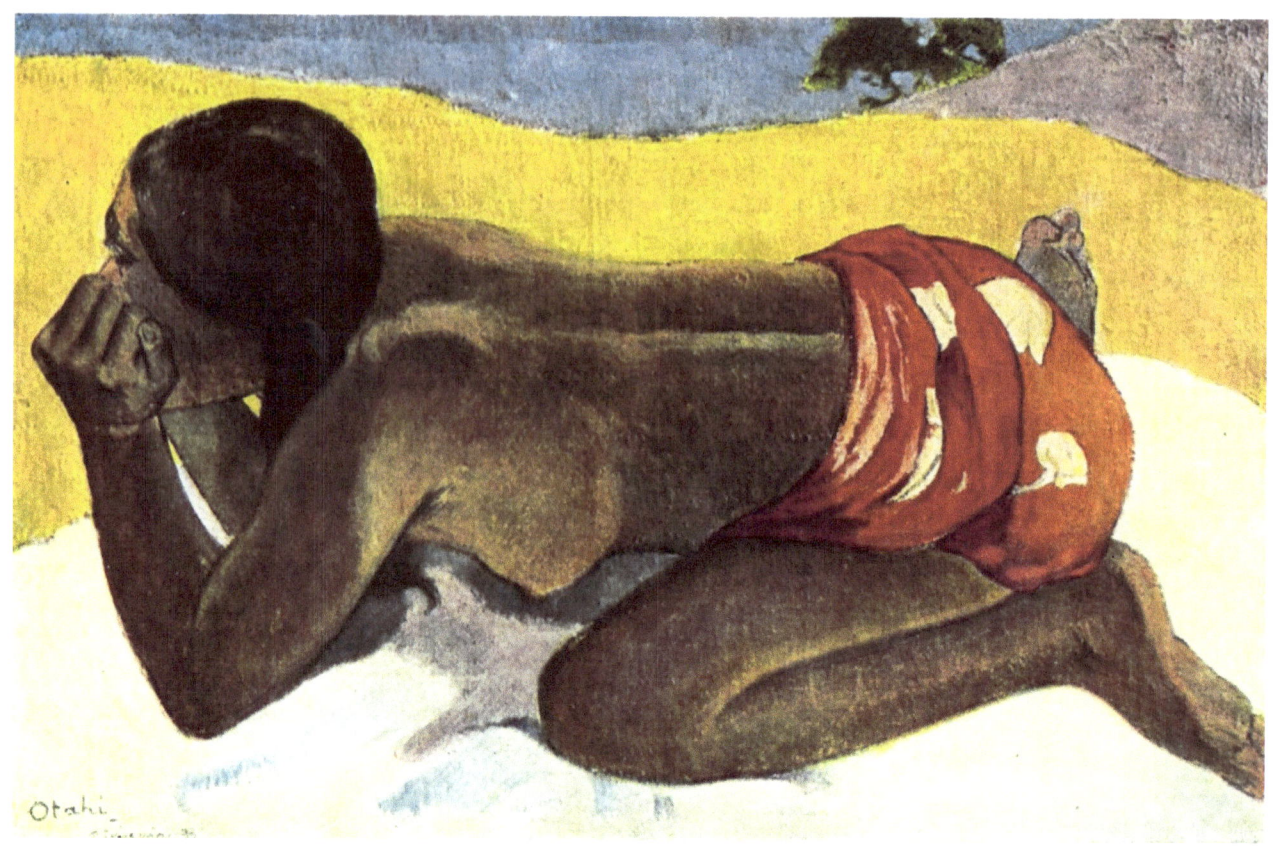

Alone—1893--French Polynesia--Cloisonnism--1st Tahiti period

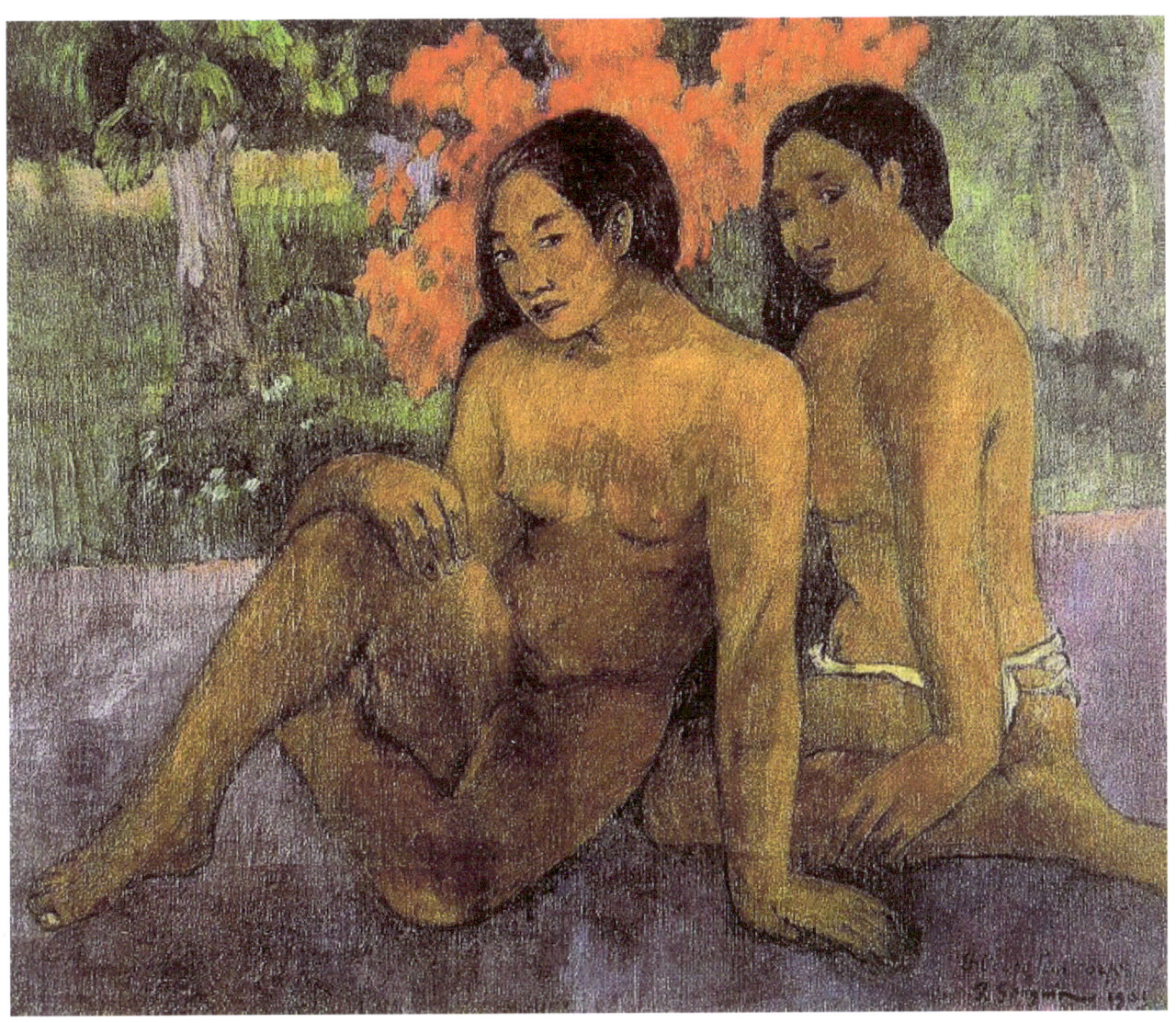

And the Gold of Their Bodies—1901--French Polynesia--Post-Impressionism--2nd Tahiti period

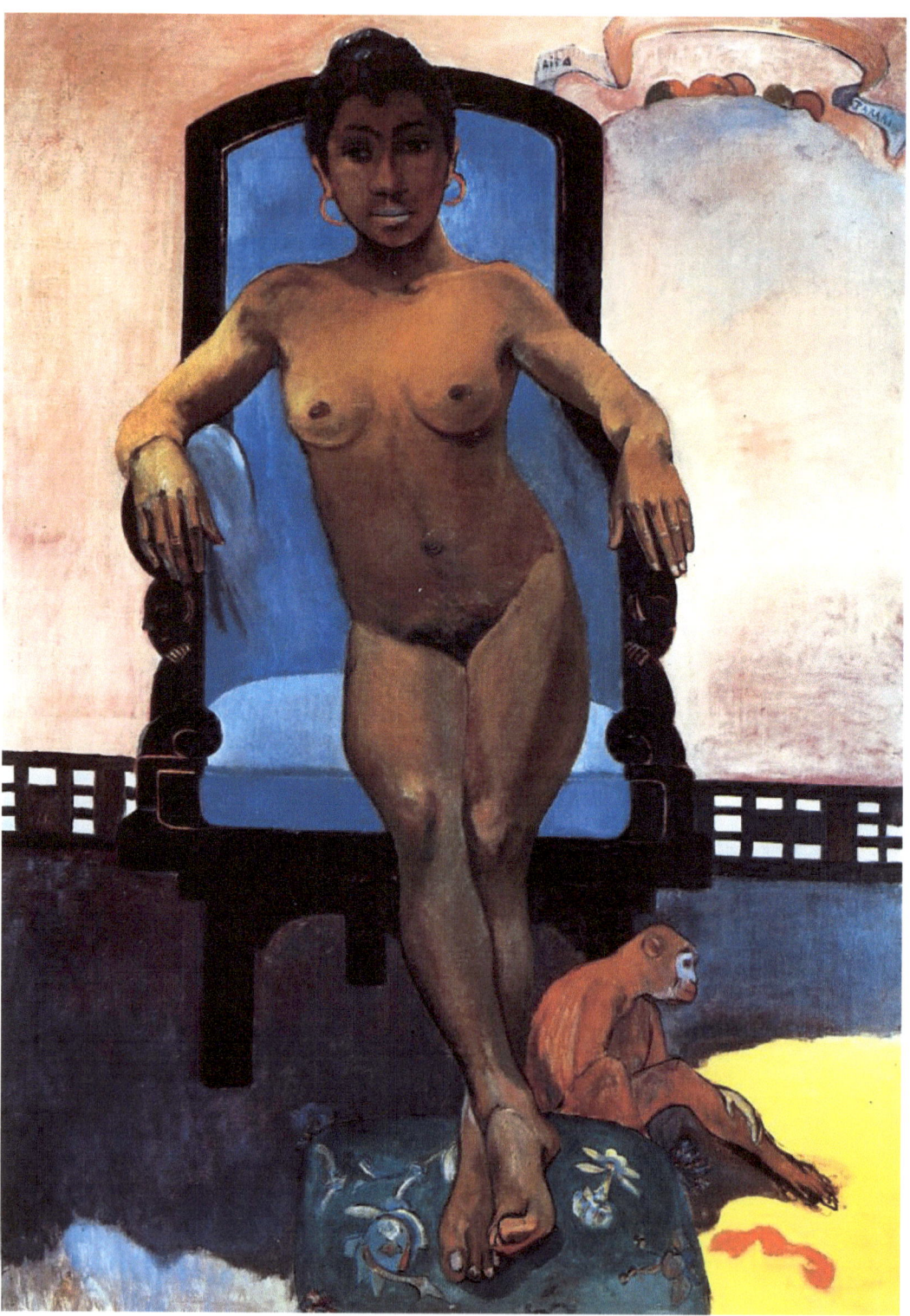

And the Gold of Their Bodies --Paul Gauguin –1901--French Polynesia--Post-Impressionism--2nd Tahiti period

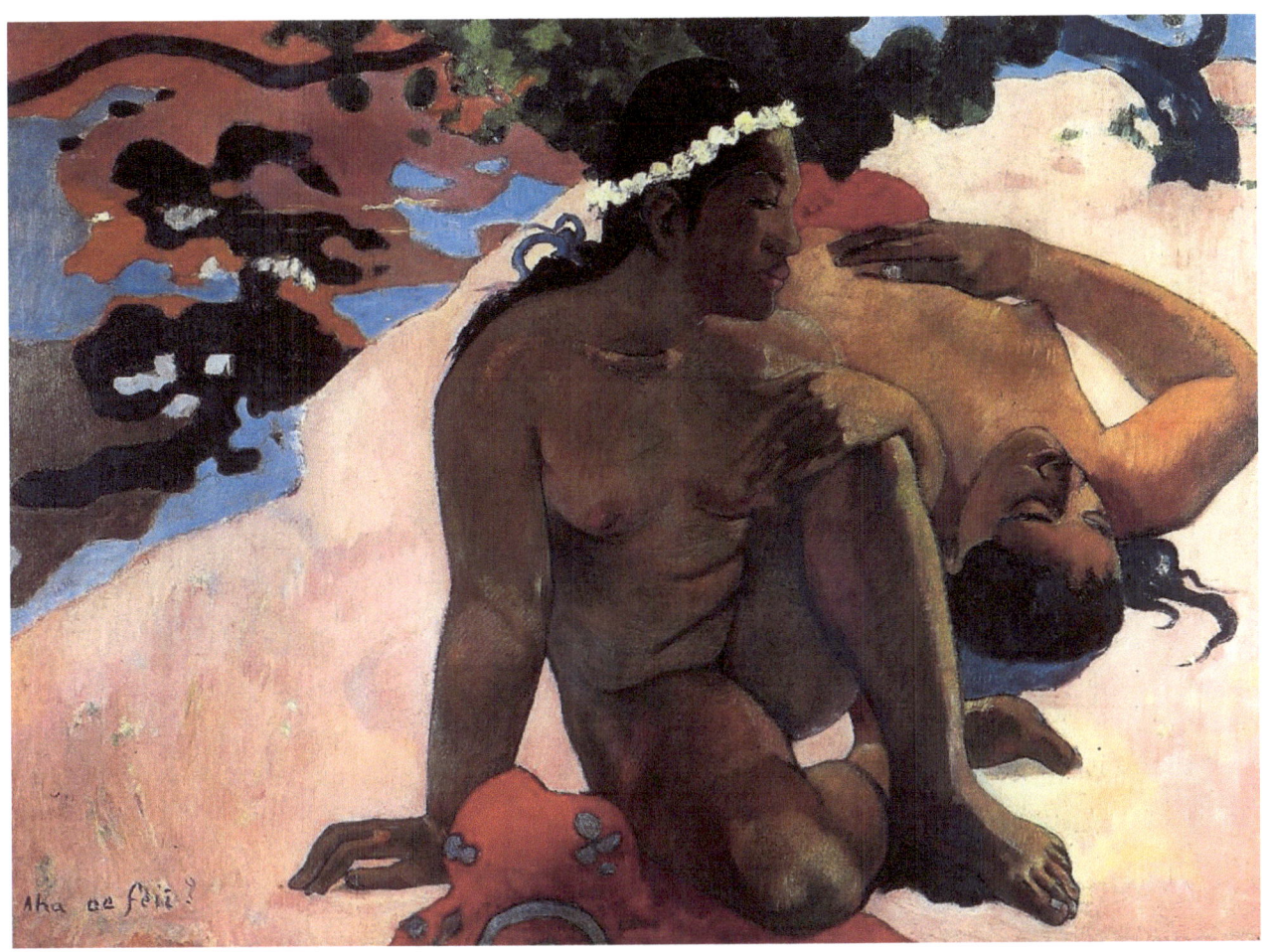

Are You Jealous?—1892--French Polynesia--Cloisonnism---1st Tahiti period

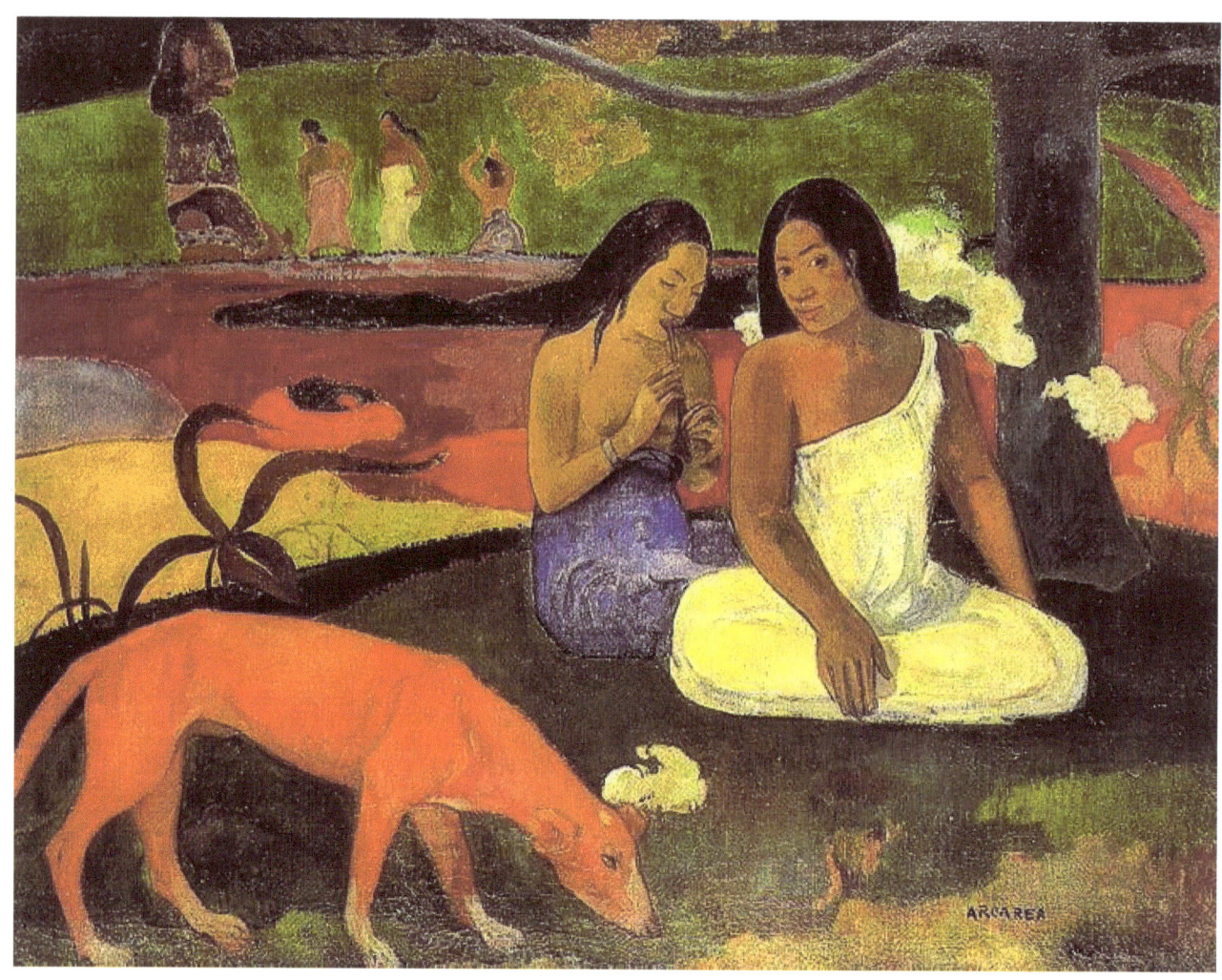

Arearea I—1892--French Polynesia--Post-Impressionism--1st Tahiti period

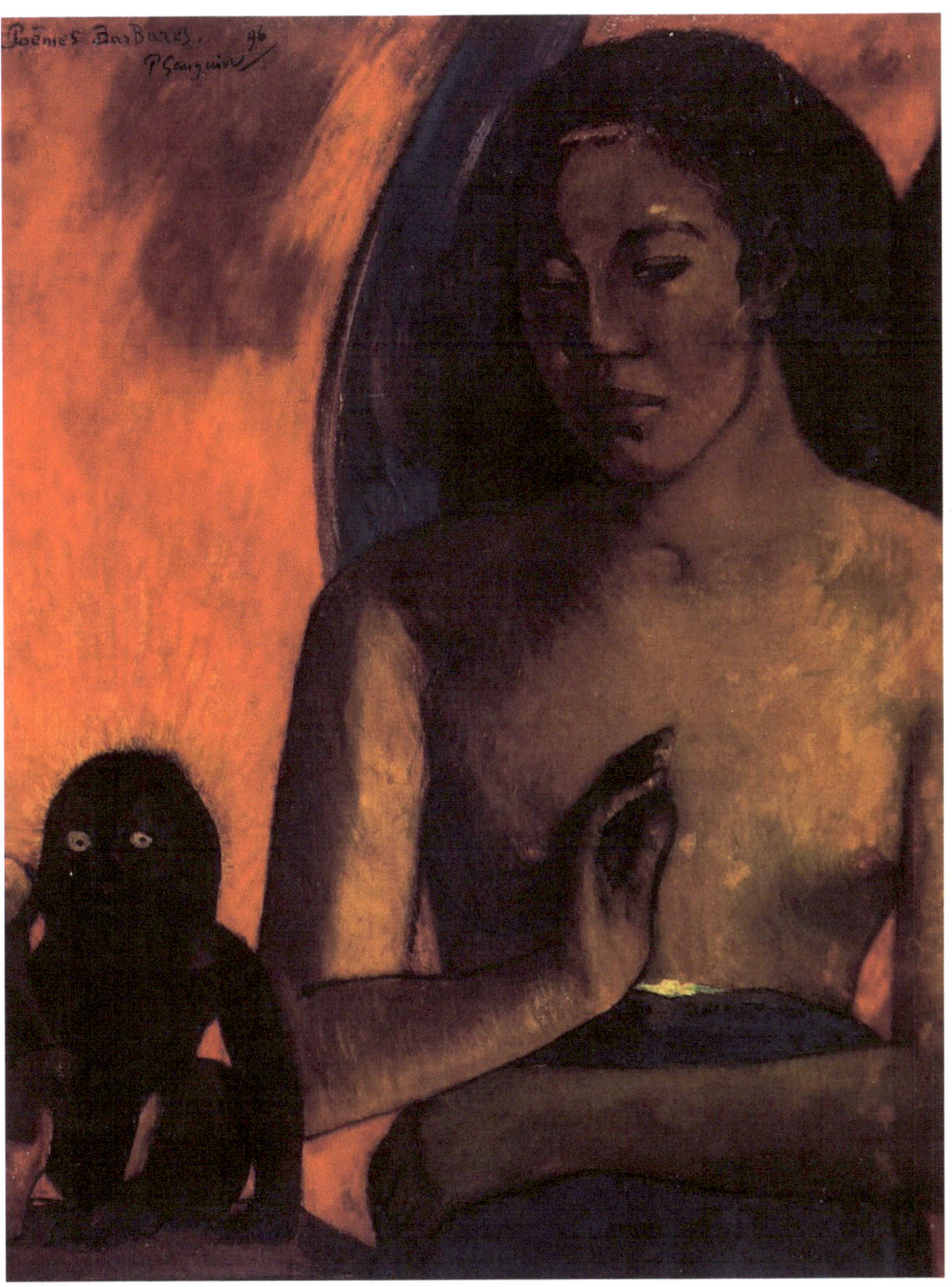

Barbarian poems—1896--French Polynesia--Cloisonnism--2nd Tahiti period

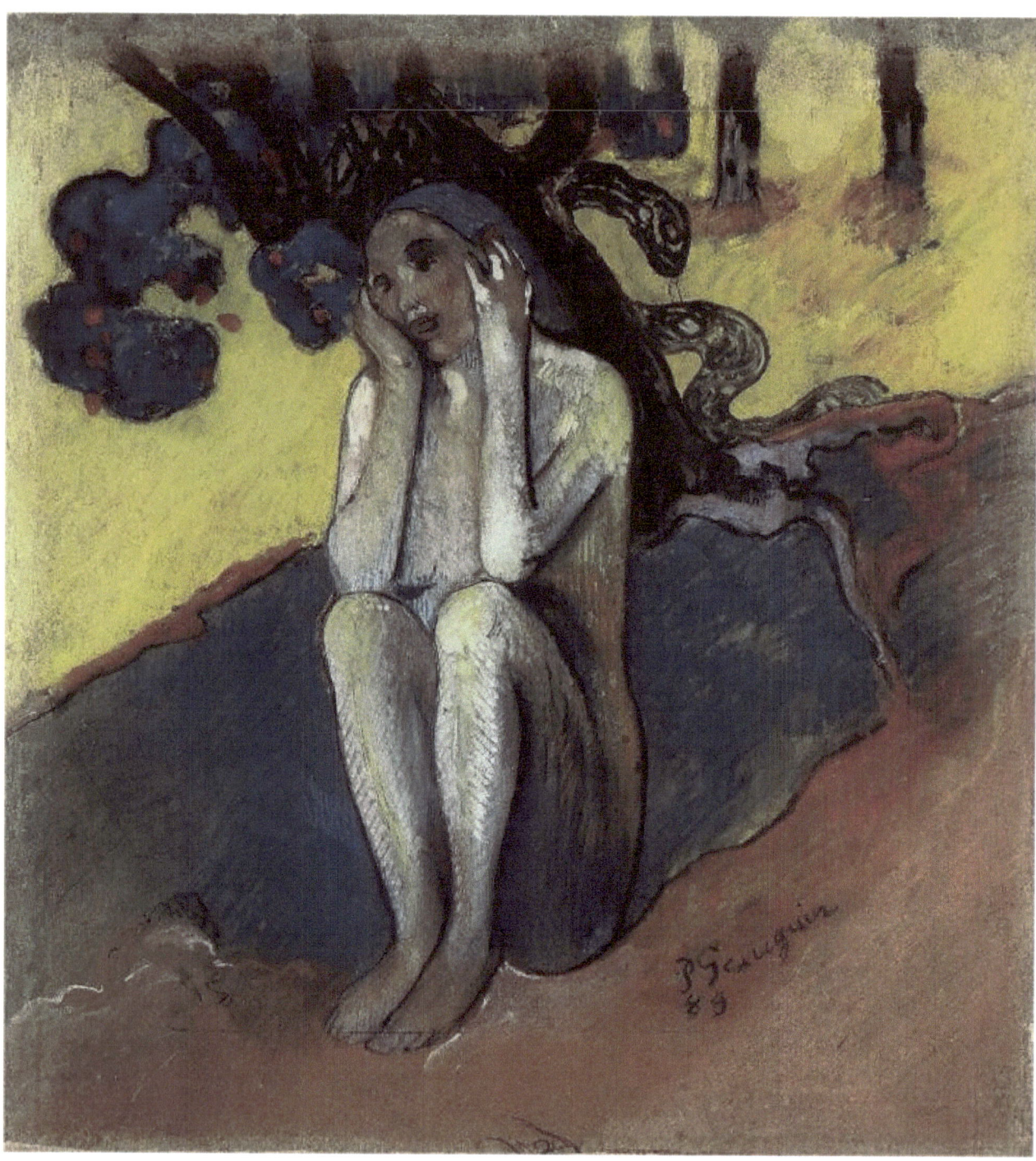

Breton Eve—1889—France--Post-Impressionism--Breton period

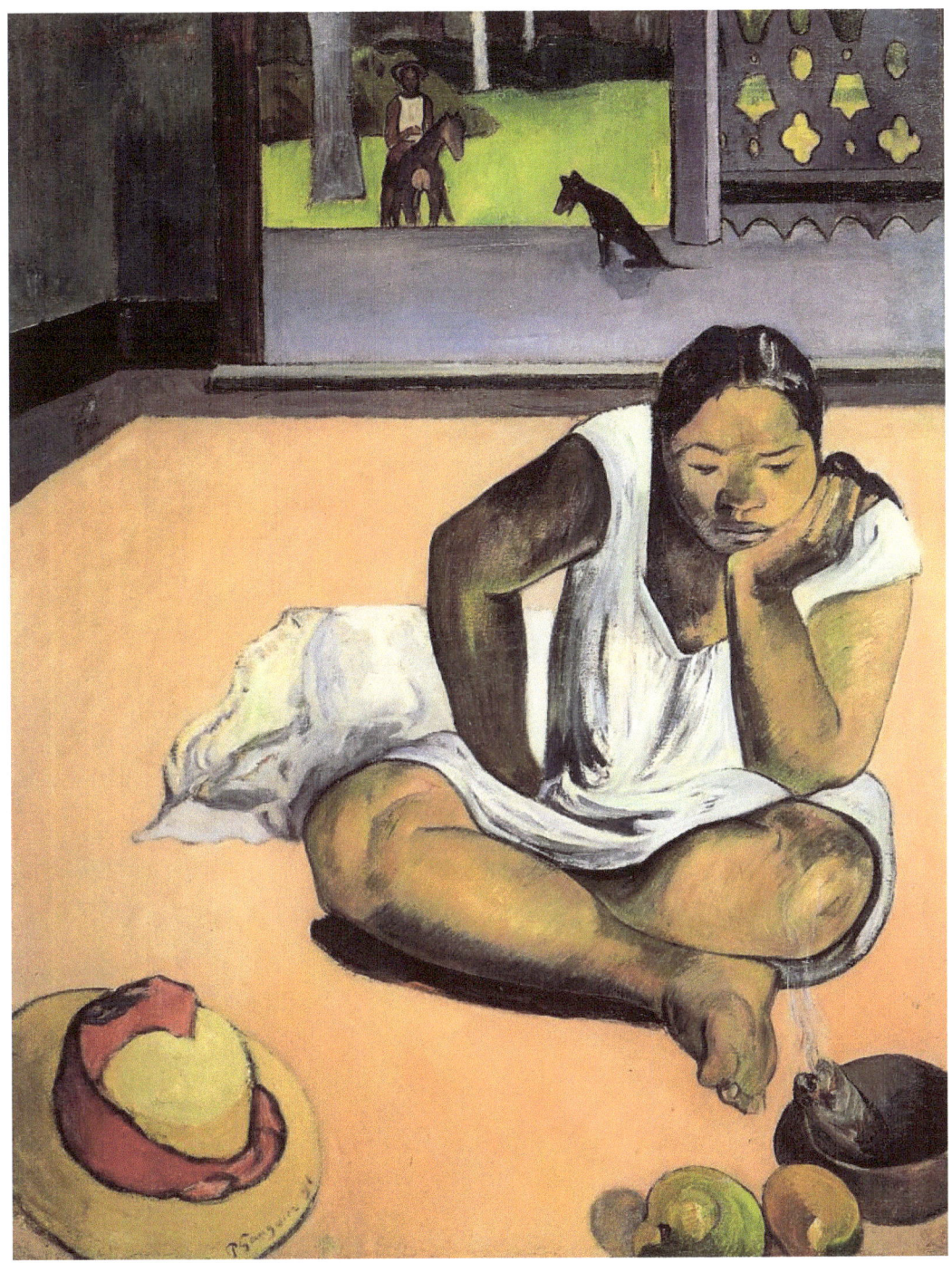

Brooding Woman—1891--French Polynesia--Cloisonnism--1st Tahiti period

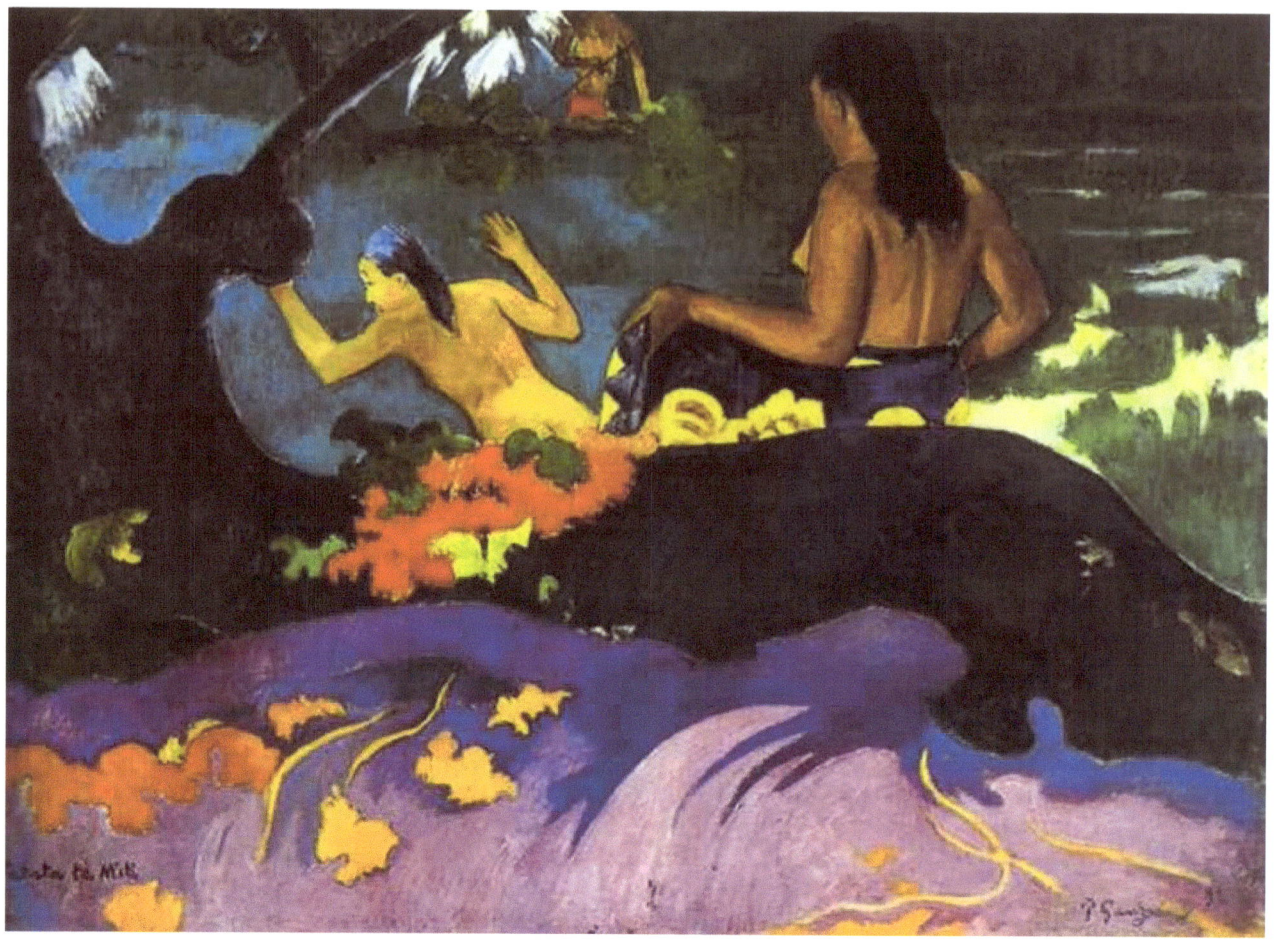

By the Sea—1892--French Polynesia--Cloisonnism--1st Tahiti period

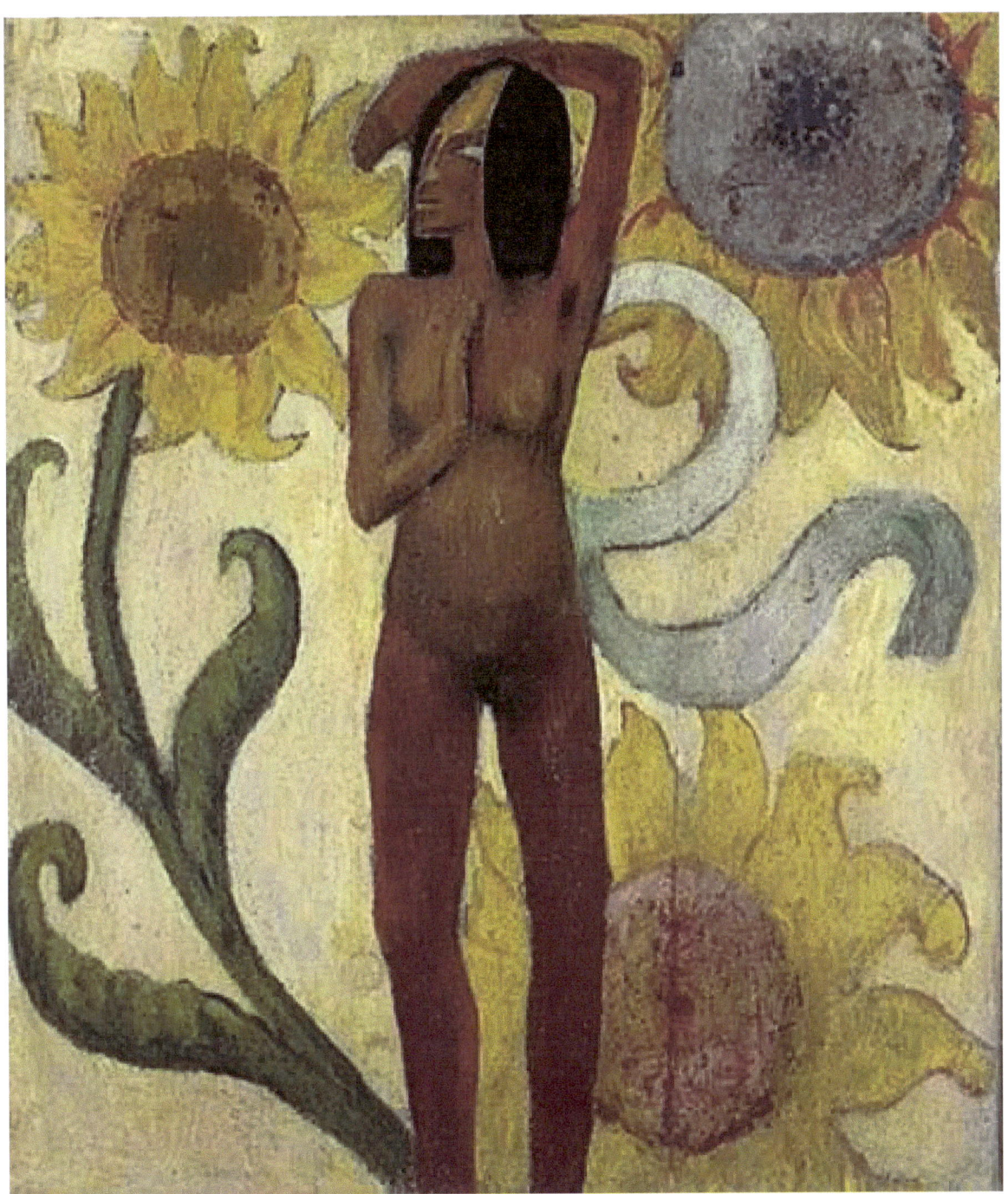

Caribbean Woman, or Female Nude with Sunflowers –1889—France--
Cloisonnism --Breton period

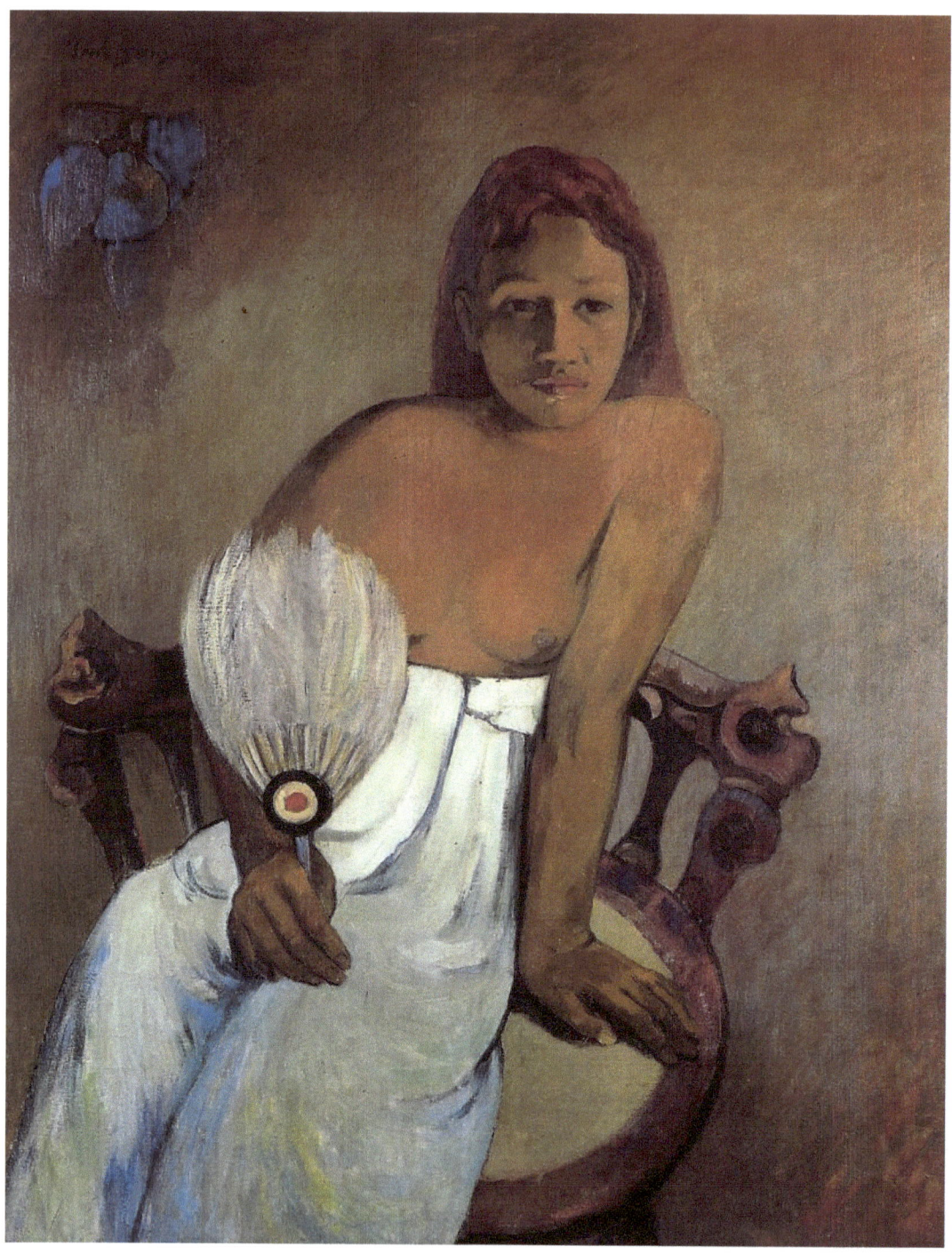

Girl with a Fan—1902--French Polynesia--Post-Impressionism--2nd Tahiti period

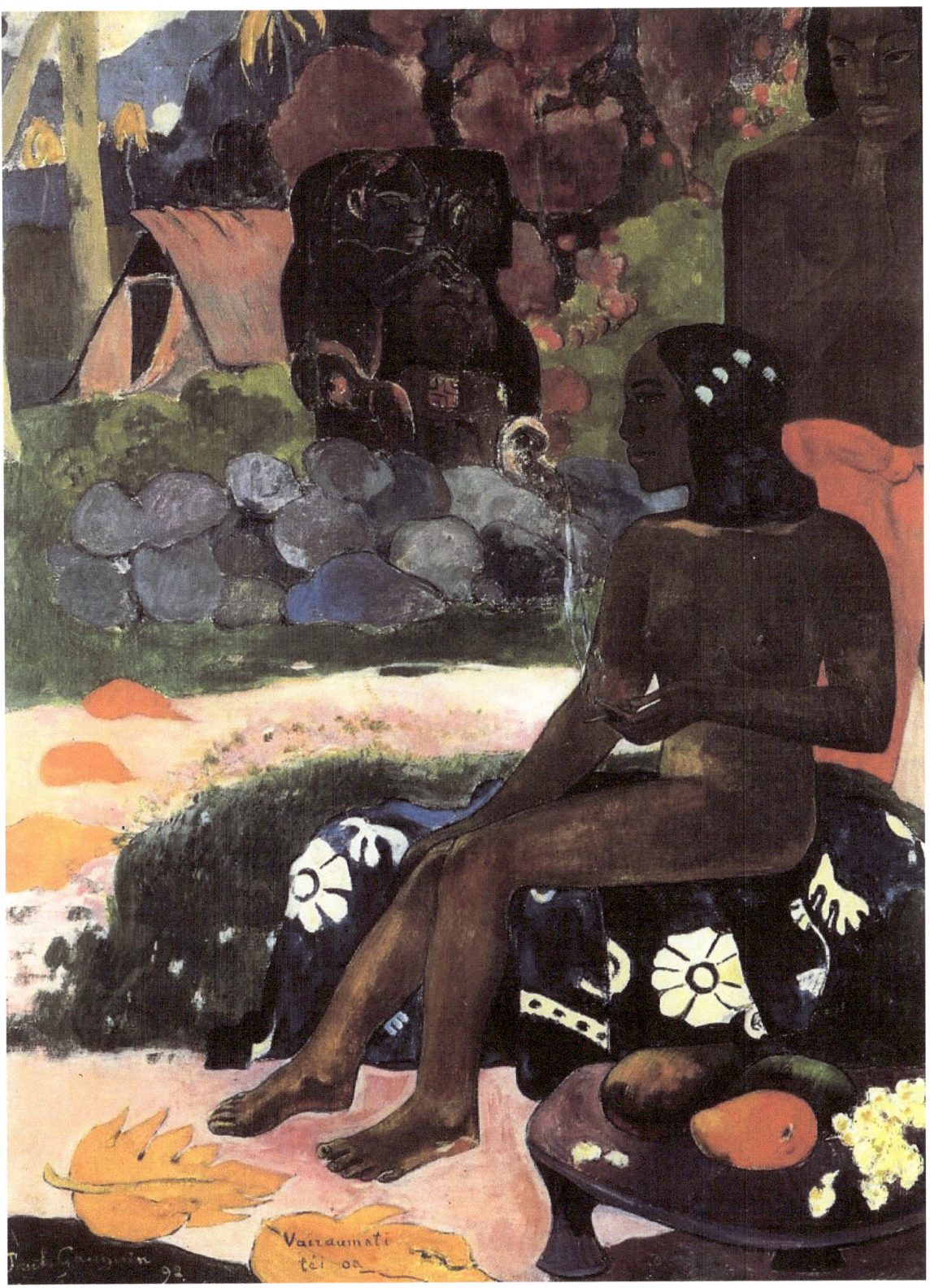

Her nami is Vairaumati –1892--French Polynesia--Post-Impressionism--
1st Tahiti period

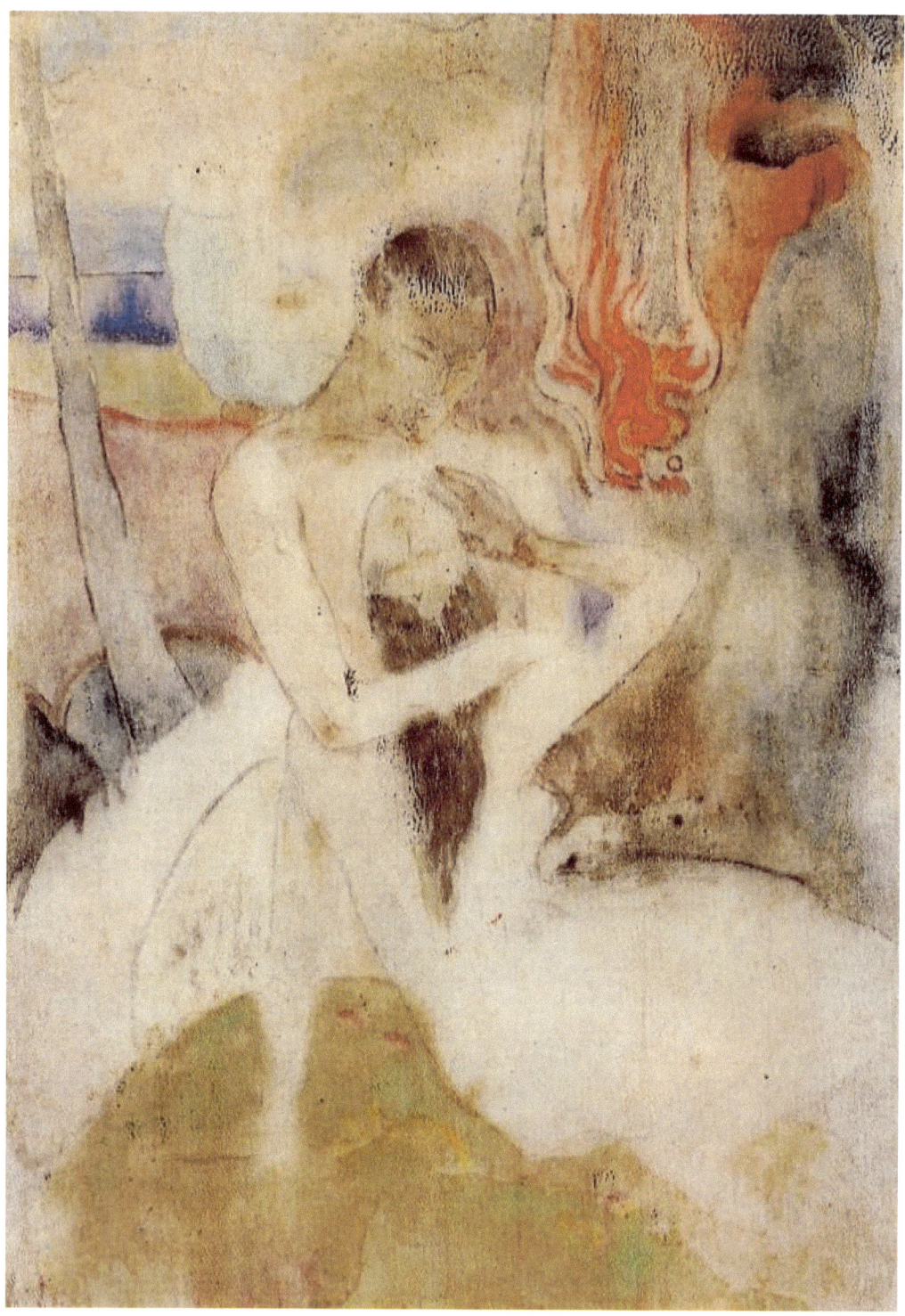

Here we make love—1893--French Polynesia--Post-Impressionism--1st Tahiti period

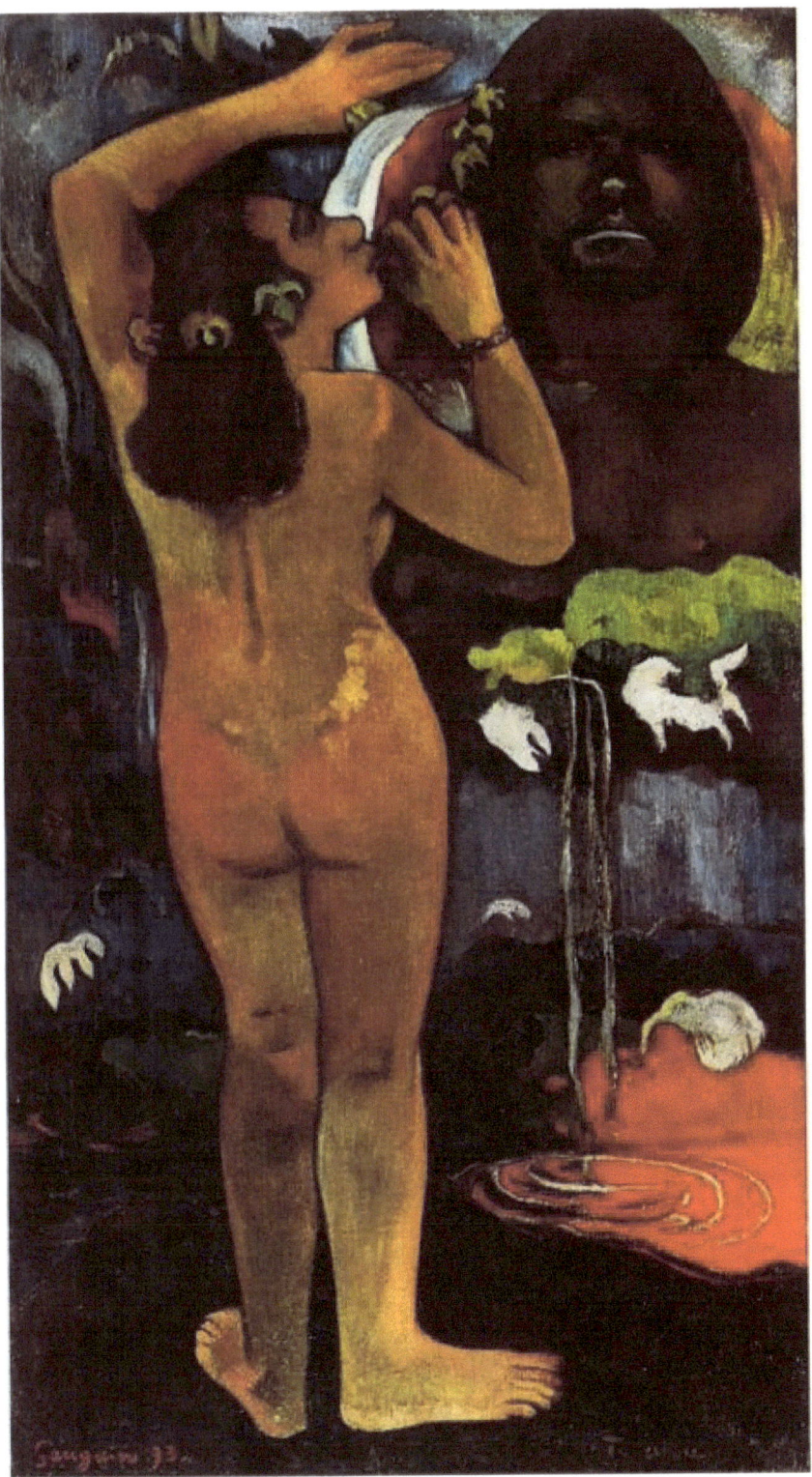

Hina, Moon Goddess & Te Fatu, Earth Spirit –1893--French Polynesia--Post-Impressionism--1st Tahiti period

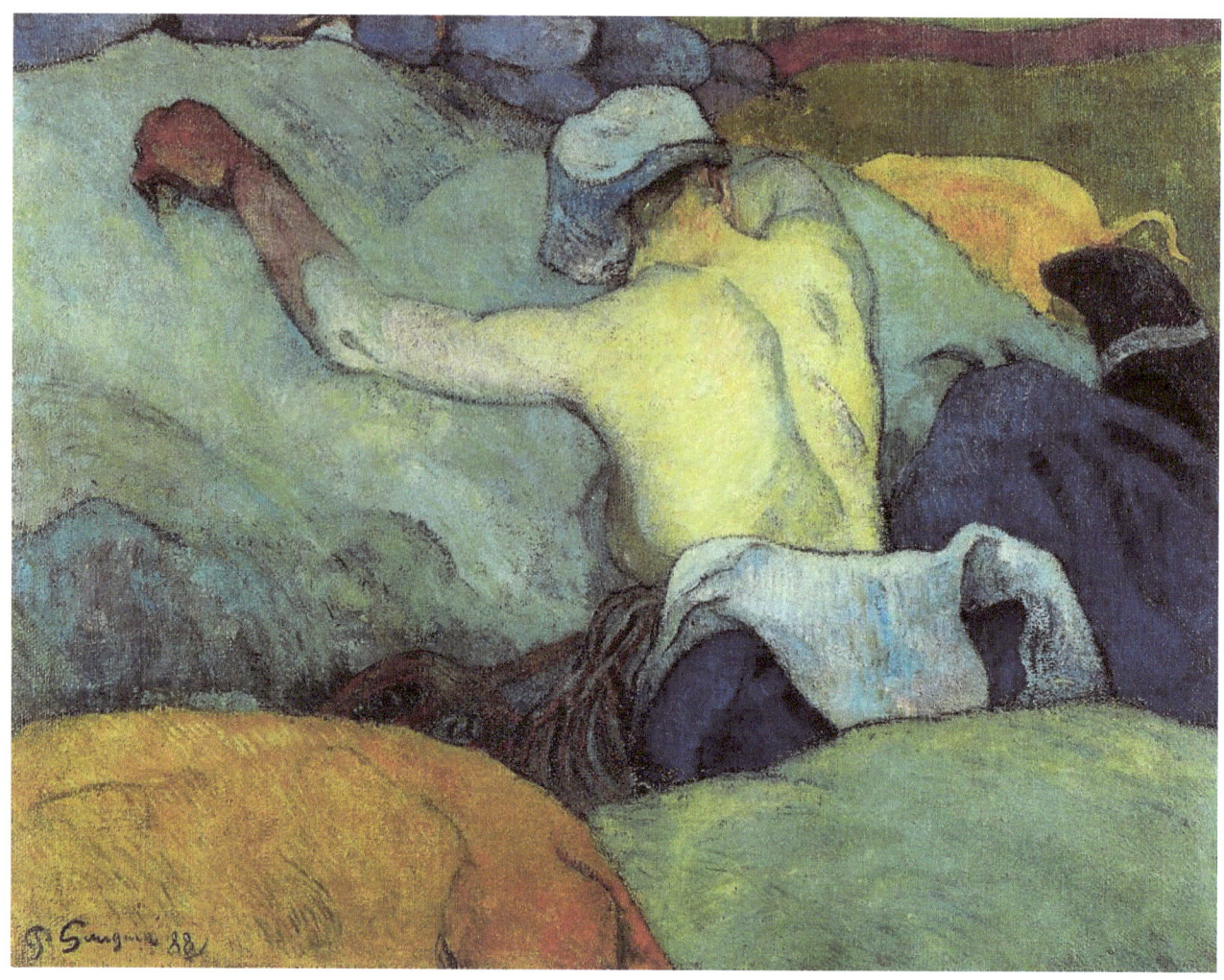

In the Heat (The Pigs) –1888—France--Post-Impressionism

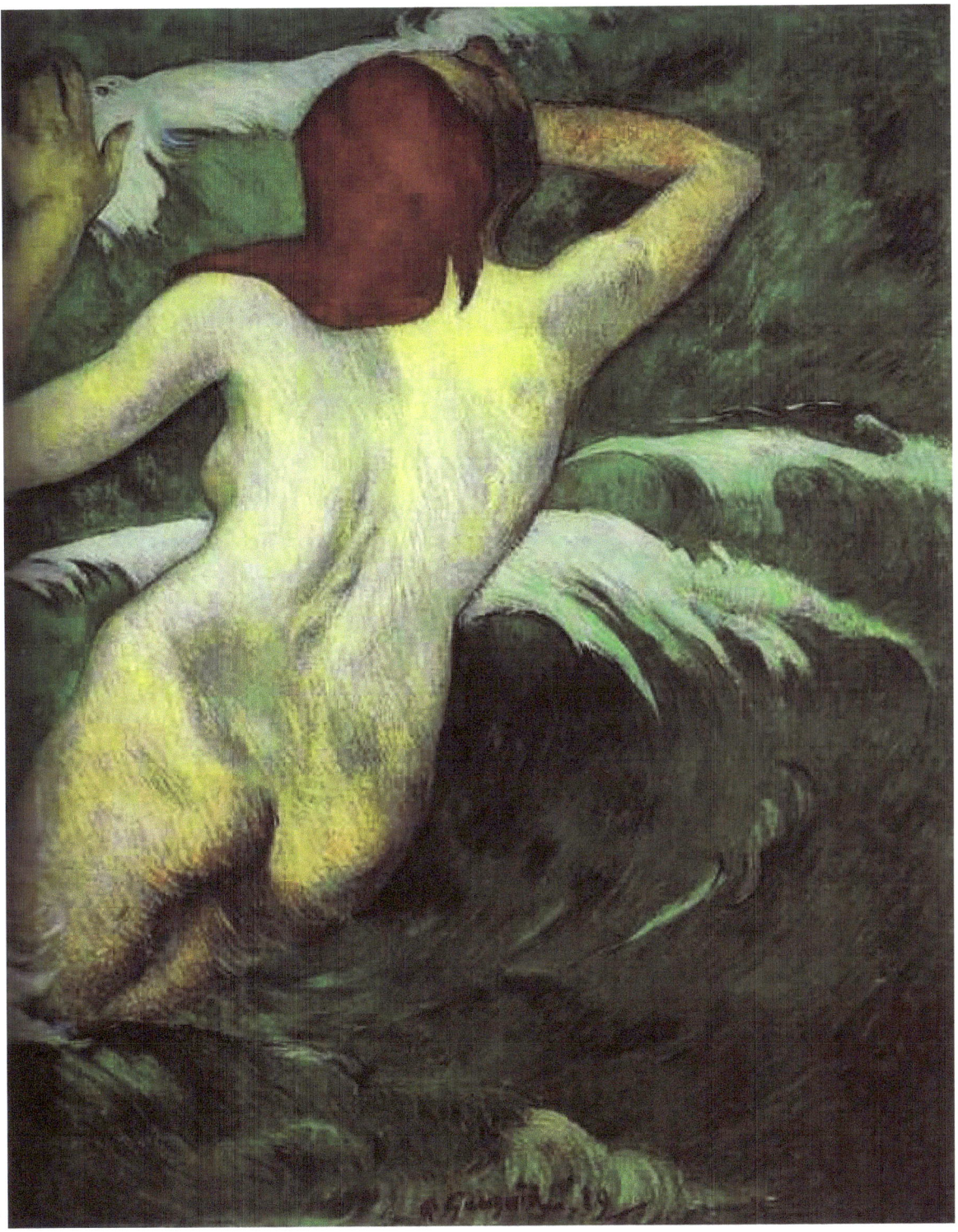

In the Waves –1889—France--Post-Impressionism--Breton period

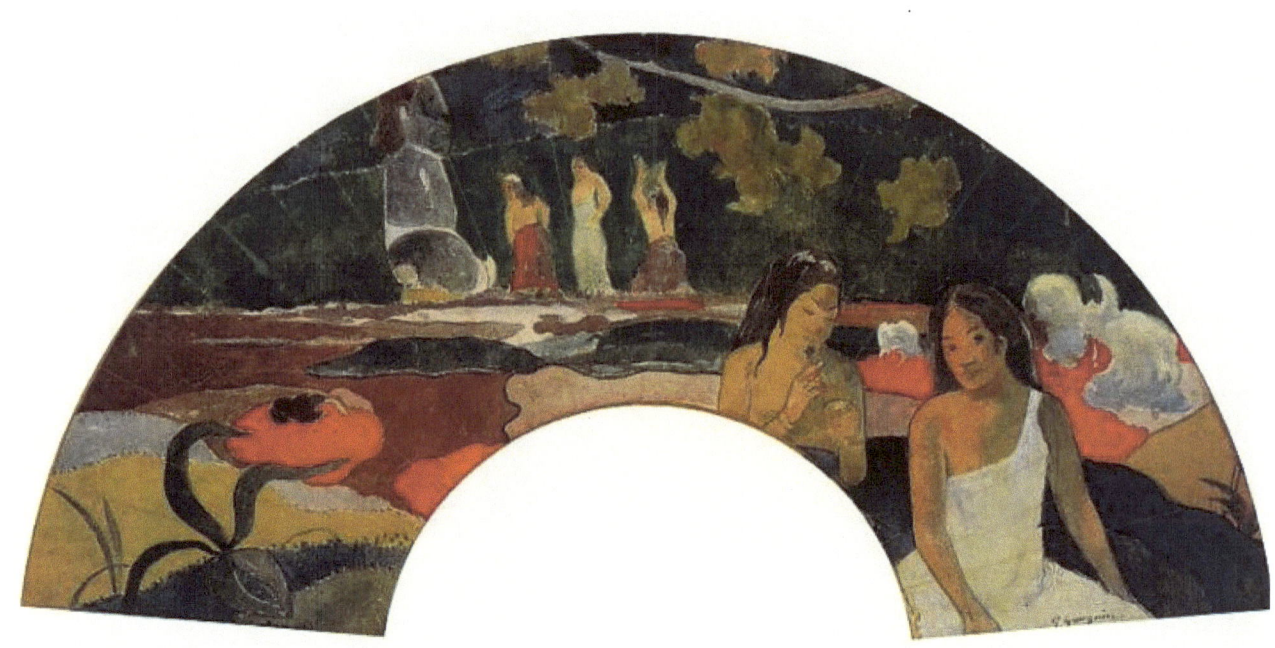

Joyousness –1892--French Polynesia--Cloisonnism--1st Tahiti period

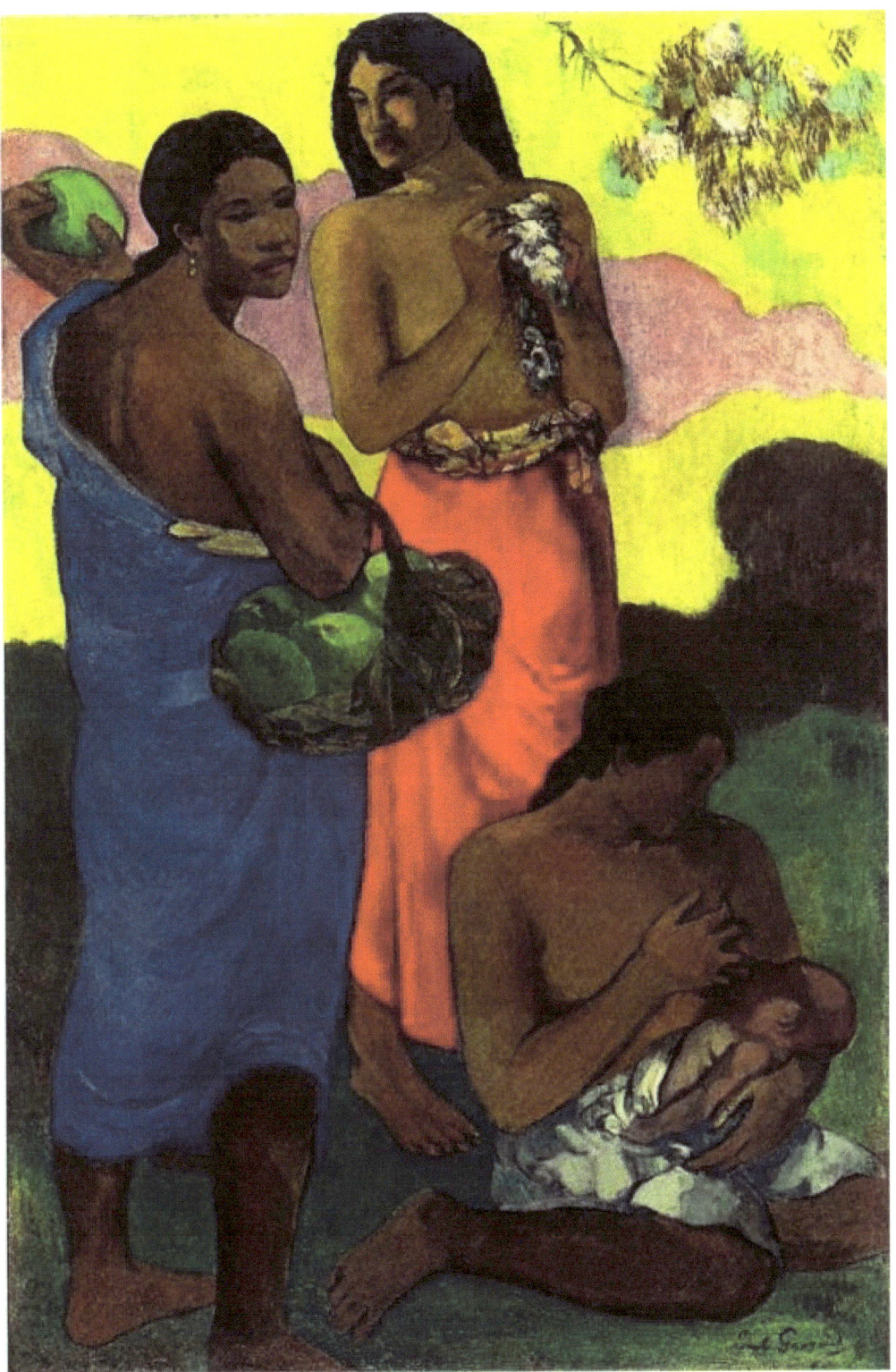

Maternite II –1899--Punaauia, French Polynesia--Post-Impressionism --2nd Tahiti period

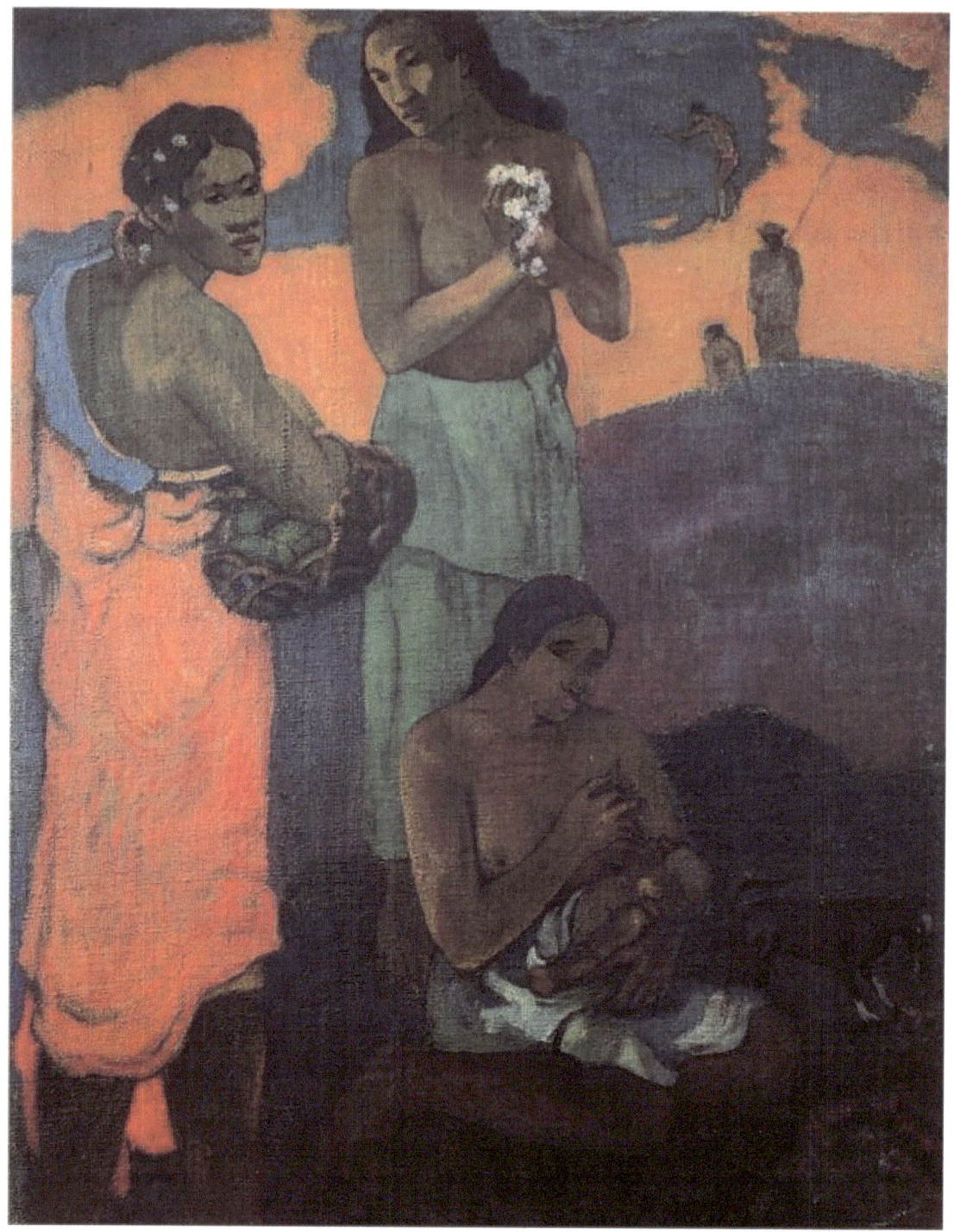

Maternity (Three Women on the Seashore) –1899--Punaauia, French—Polynesia--
Cloisonnism--2nd Tahiti period

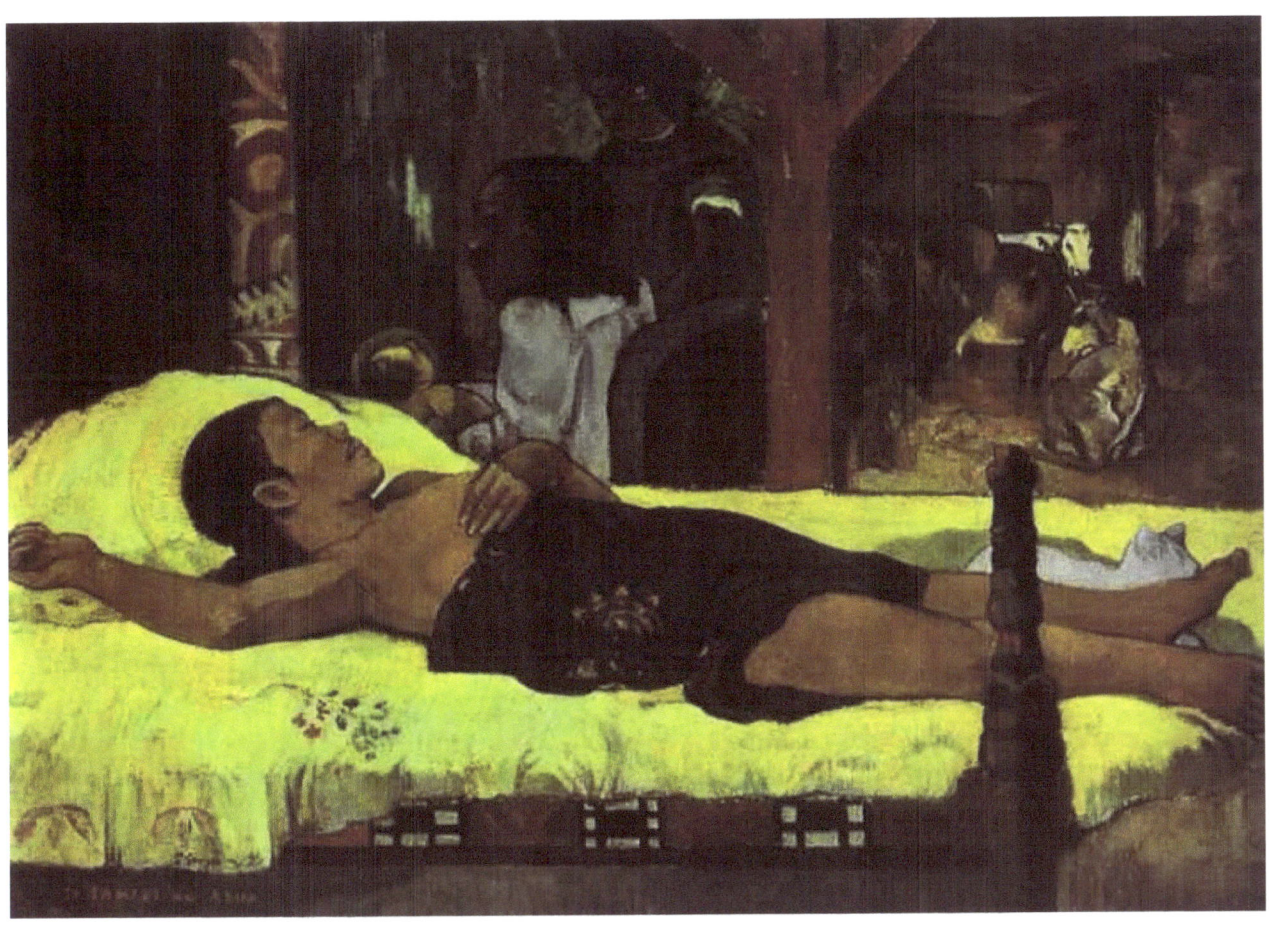

Nativity—1896--French Polynesia--Post-Impressionism --2nd Tahiti period

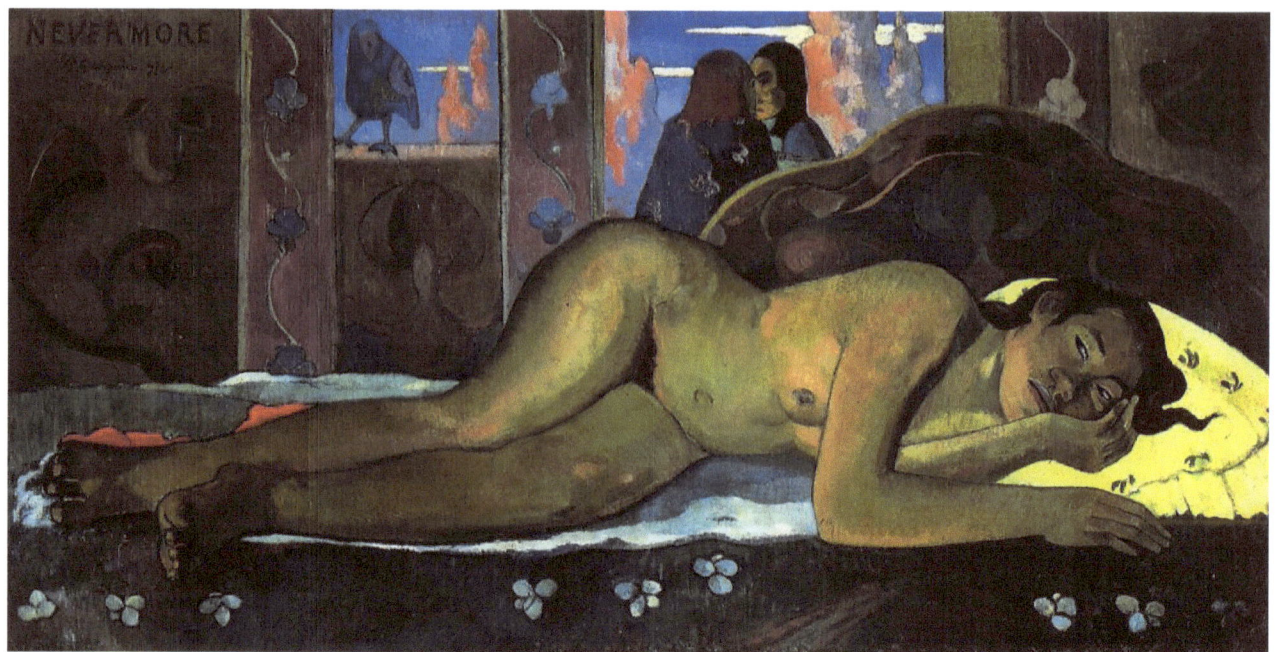

Nevermore –1897--Punaauia, French Polynesia--Post-Impressionism--2nd Tahiti
period

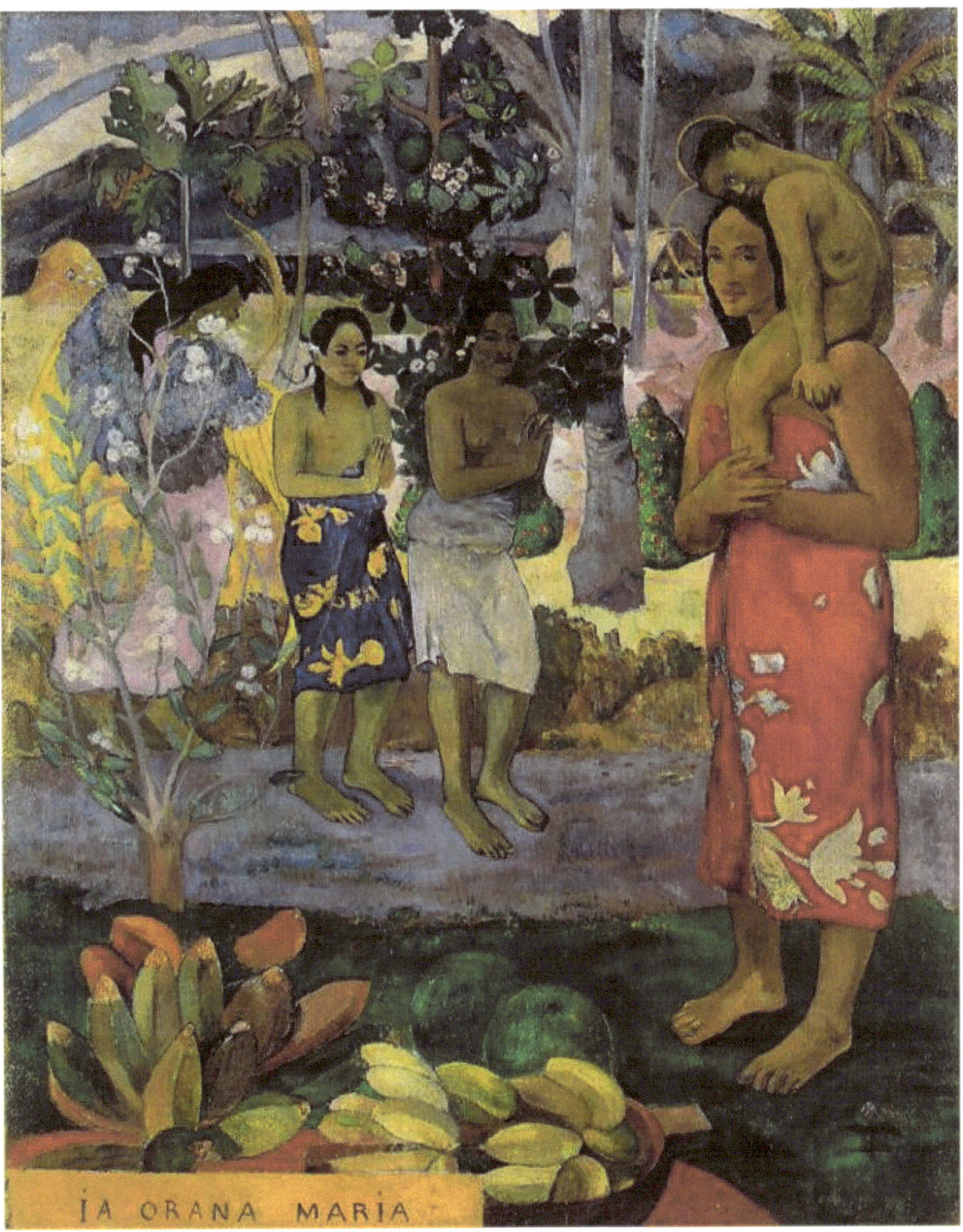

Orana Maria (We Hail Thee Mary)—1891--French Polynesia--Cloisonnism--
1st Tahiti period

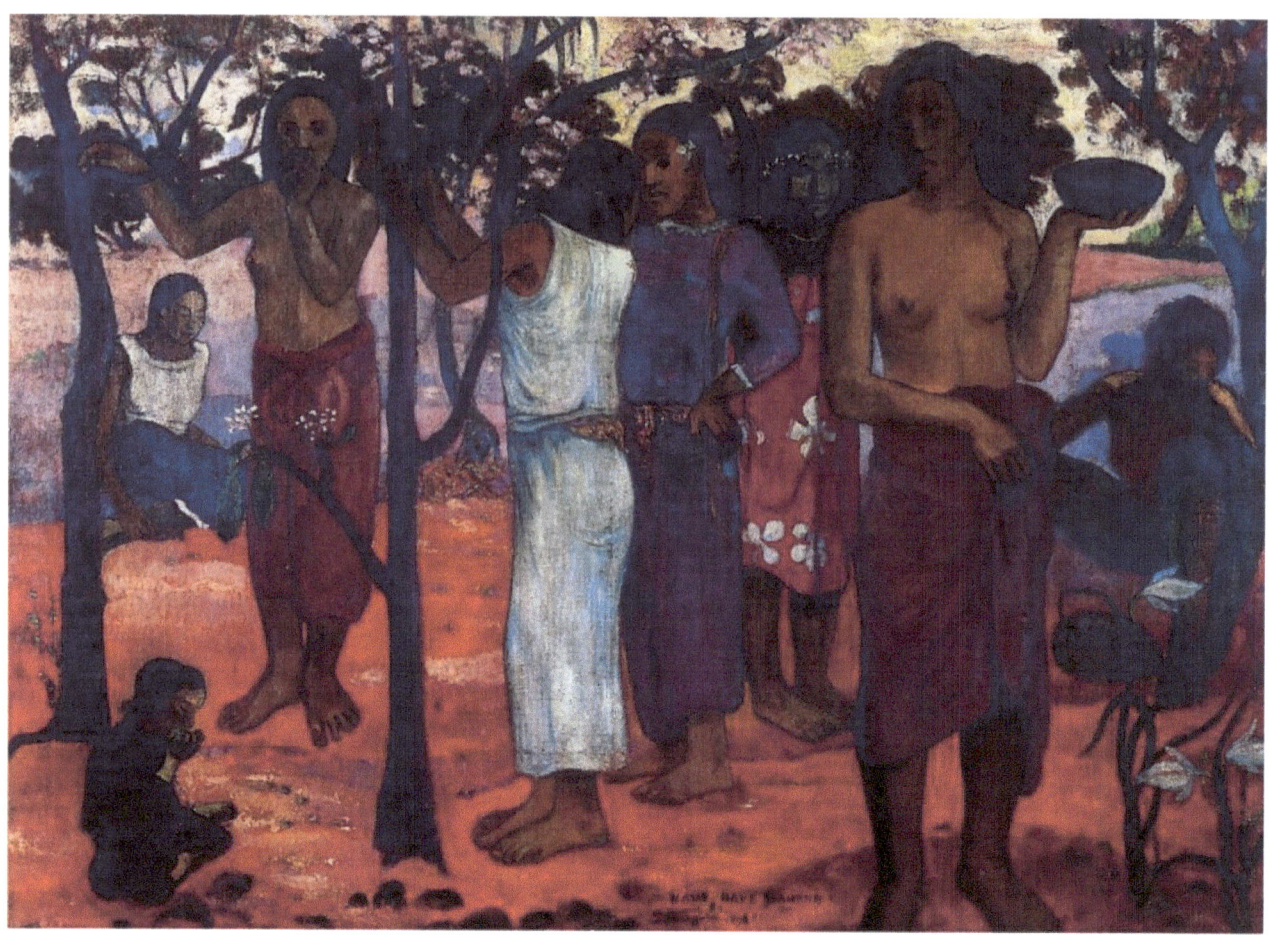

Perfect days—1896--Post-Impressionism--2nd Tahiti period

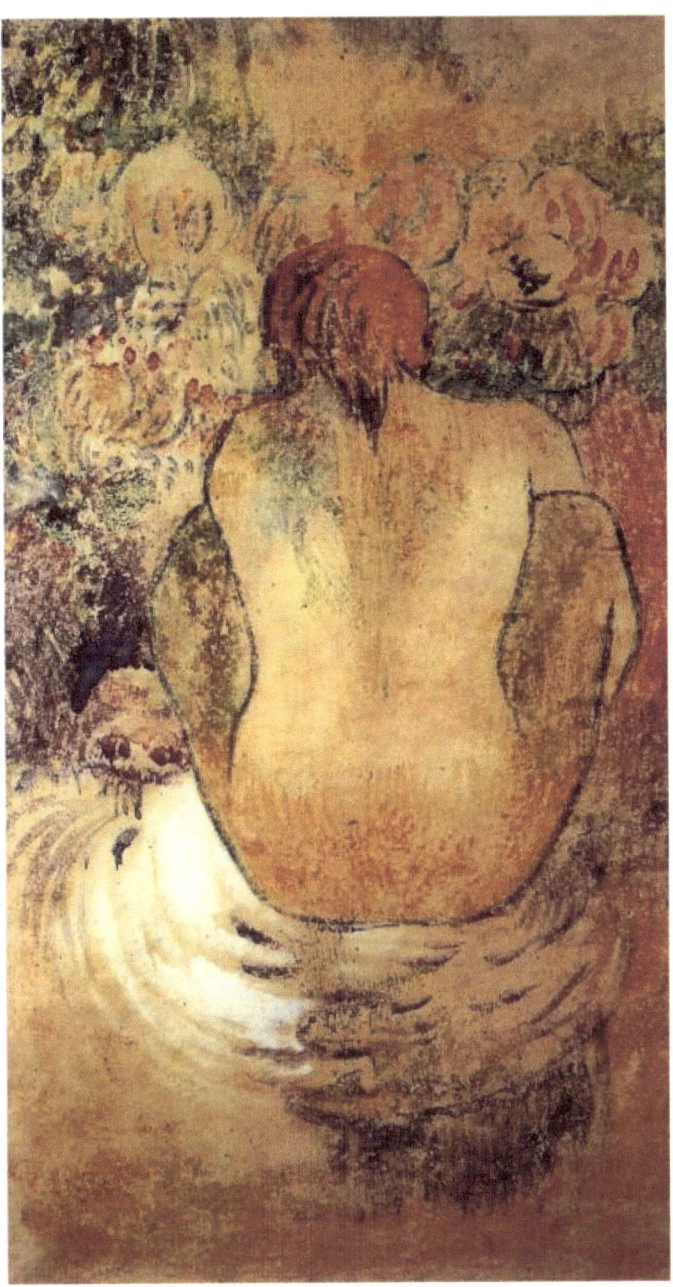

Crouching Tahitian woman—1902--French Polynesia--Post-Impressionism --2nd
Tahiti period

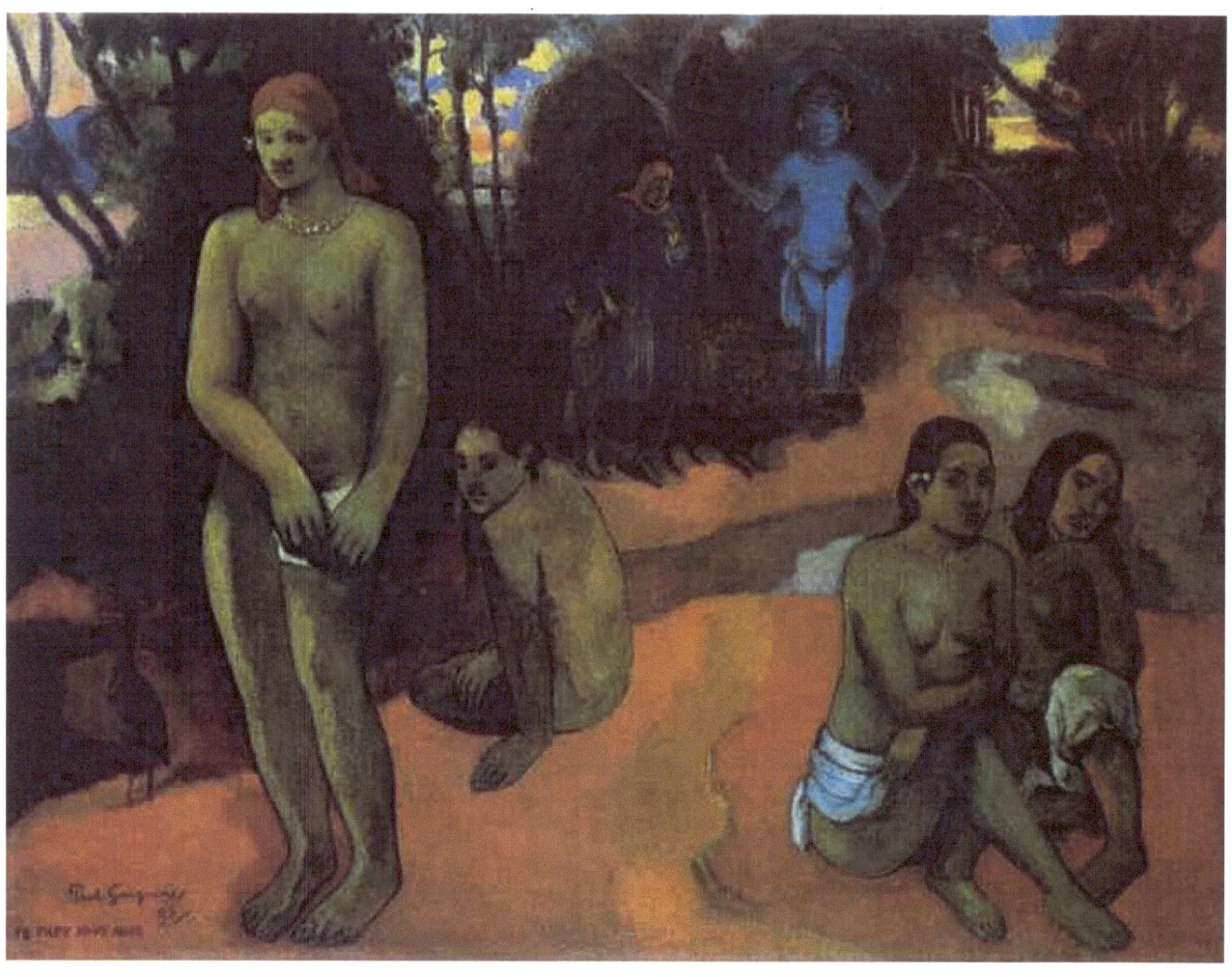

Delectable Waters—1898--French Polynesia--Cloisonnism--2nd Tahiti period

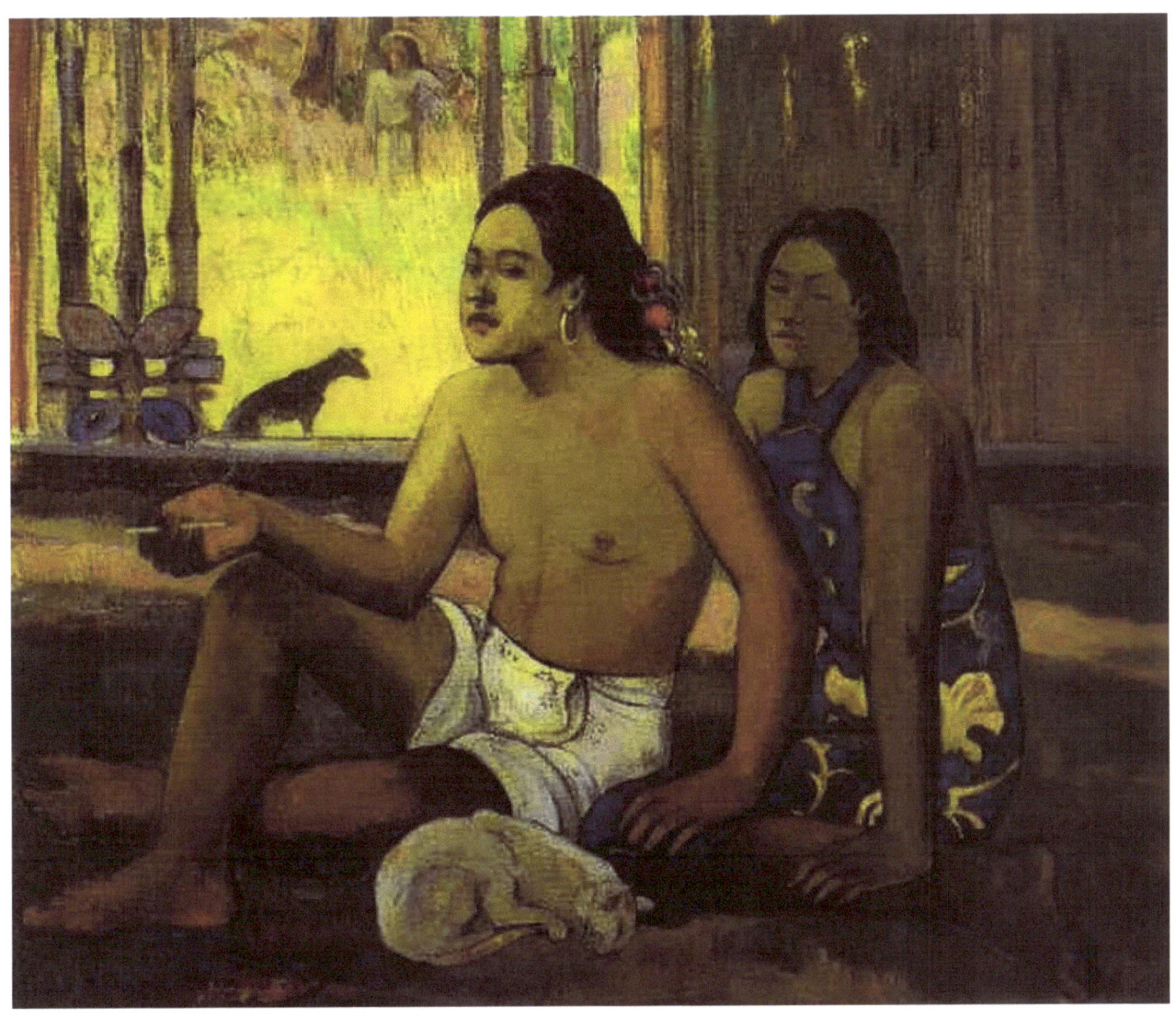

Eiaha Ohipa or Tahitians in a Room—1896--French Polynesia--Cloisonnism--2nd
Tahiti period

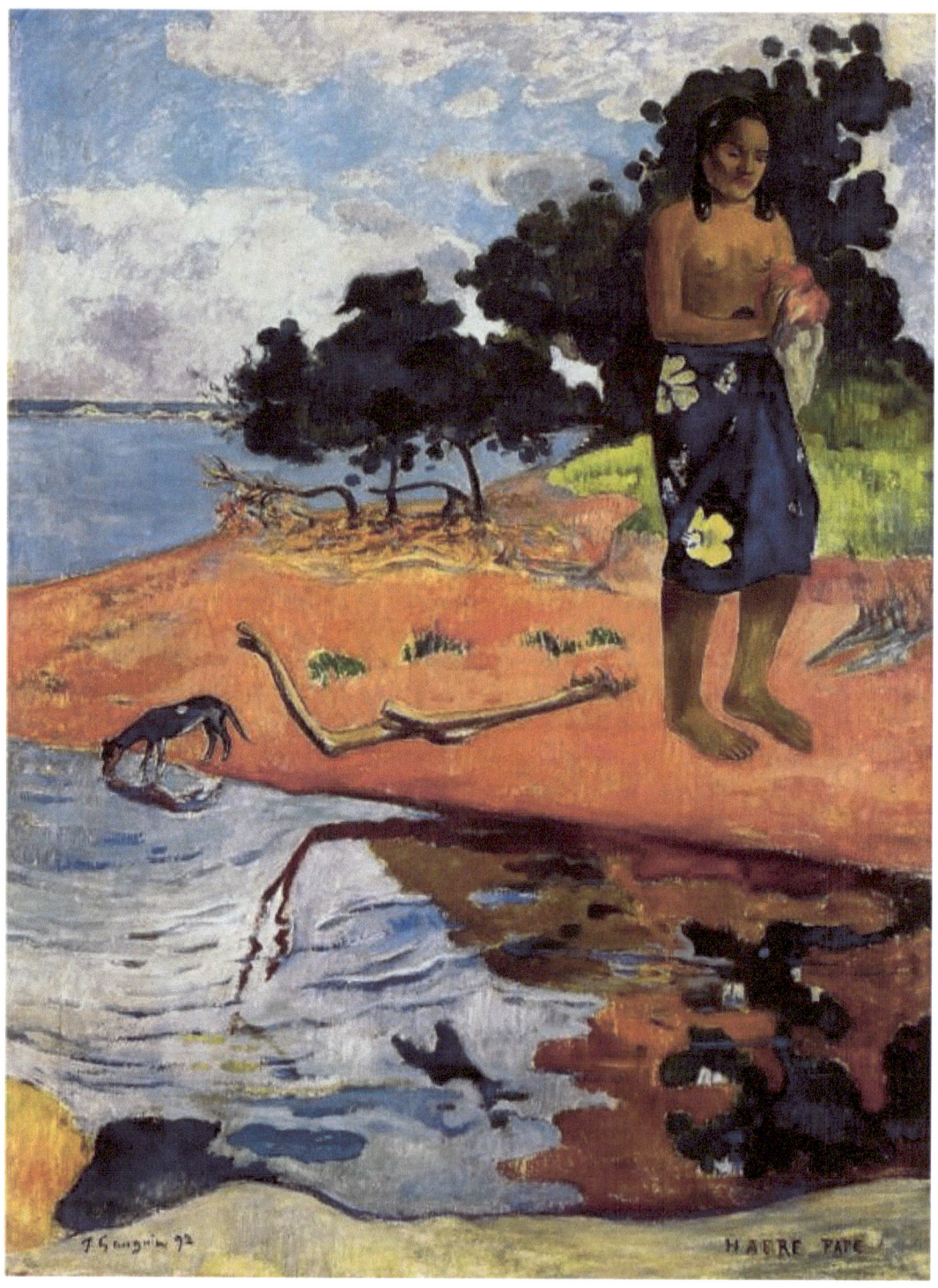

She goes down to the fresh water (Haere Pape)—1892--French Polynesia

Cloisonnism--1st Tahiti period

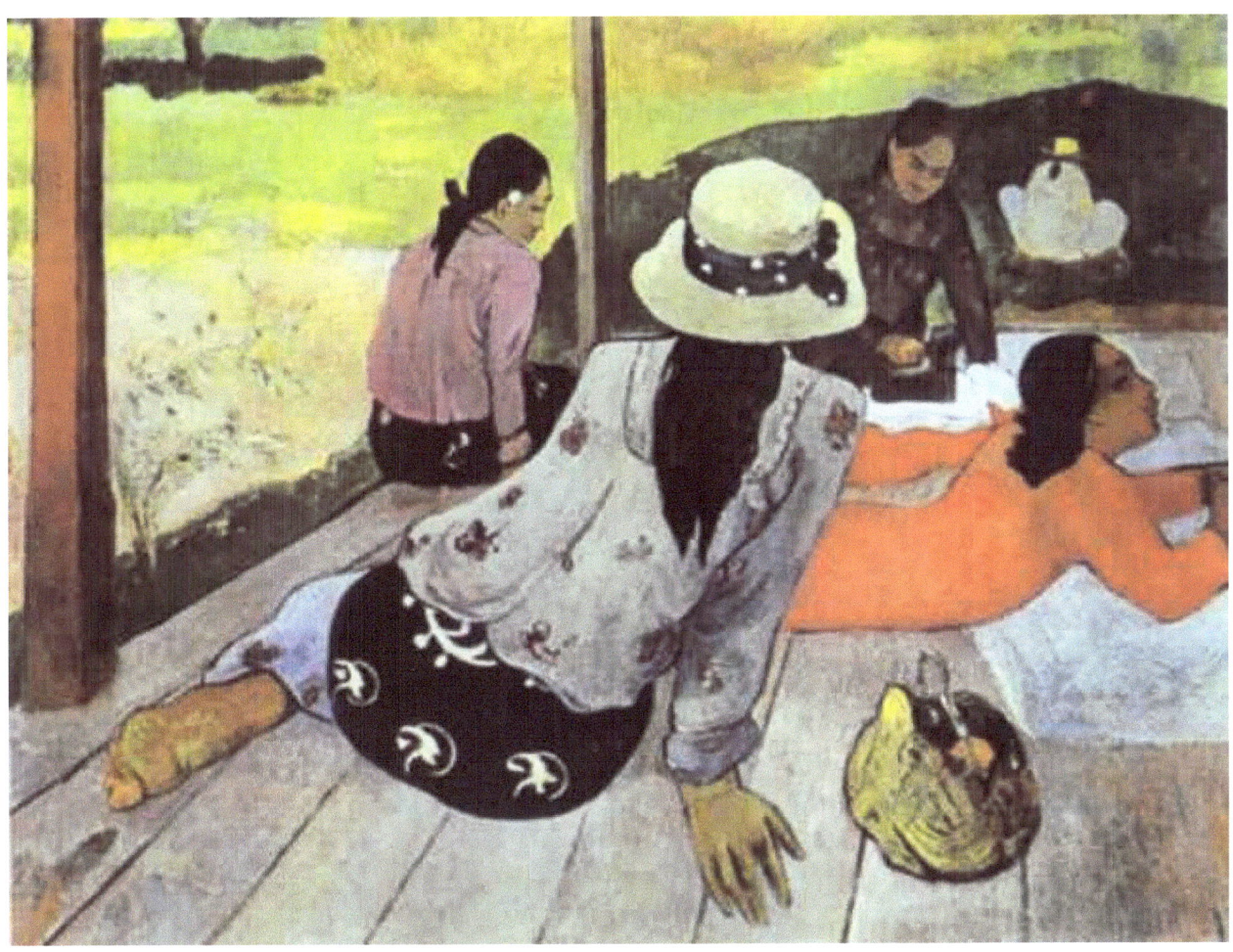

Siesta—1894--Place of Creation: Paris, Fran--Post-Impressionism

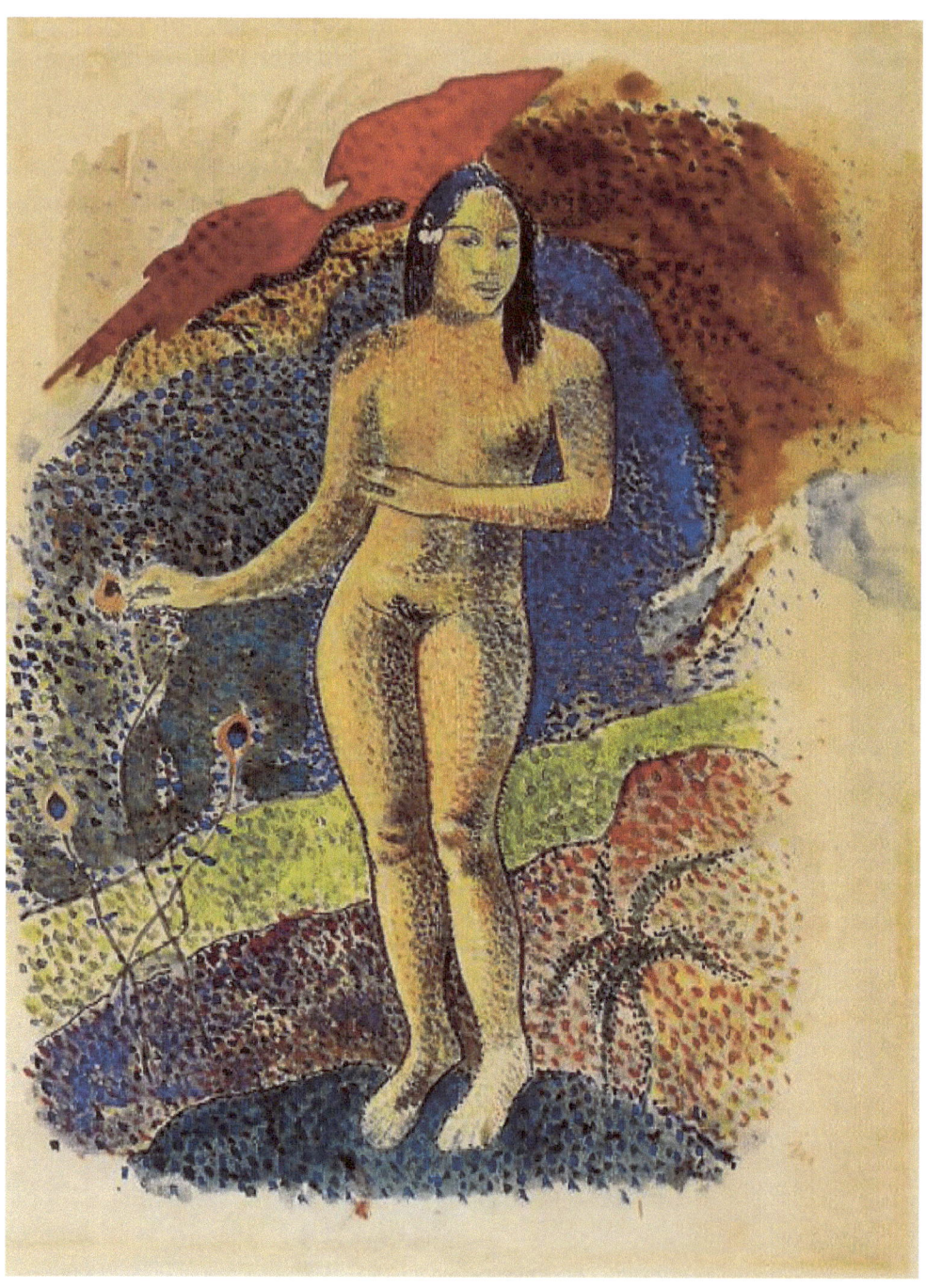

Tahitian Eve –1892--French Polynesia--Post-Impressionism--1st Tahiti period

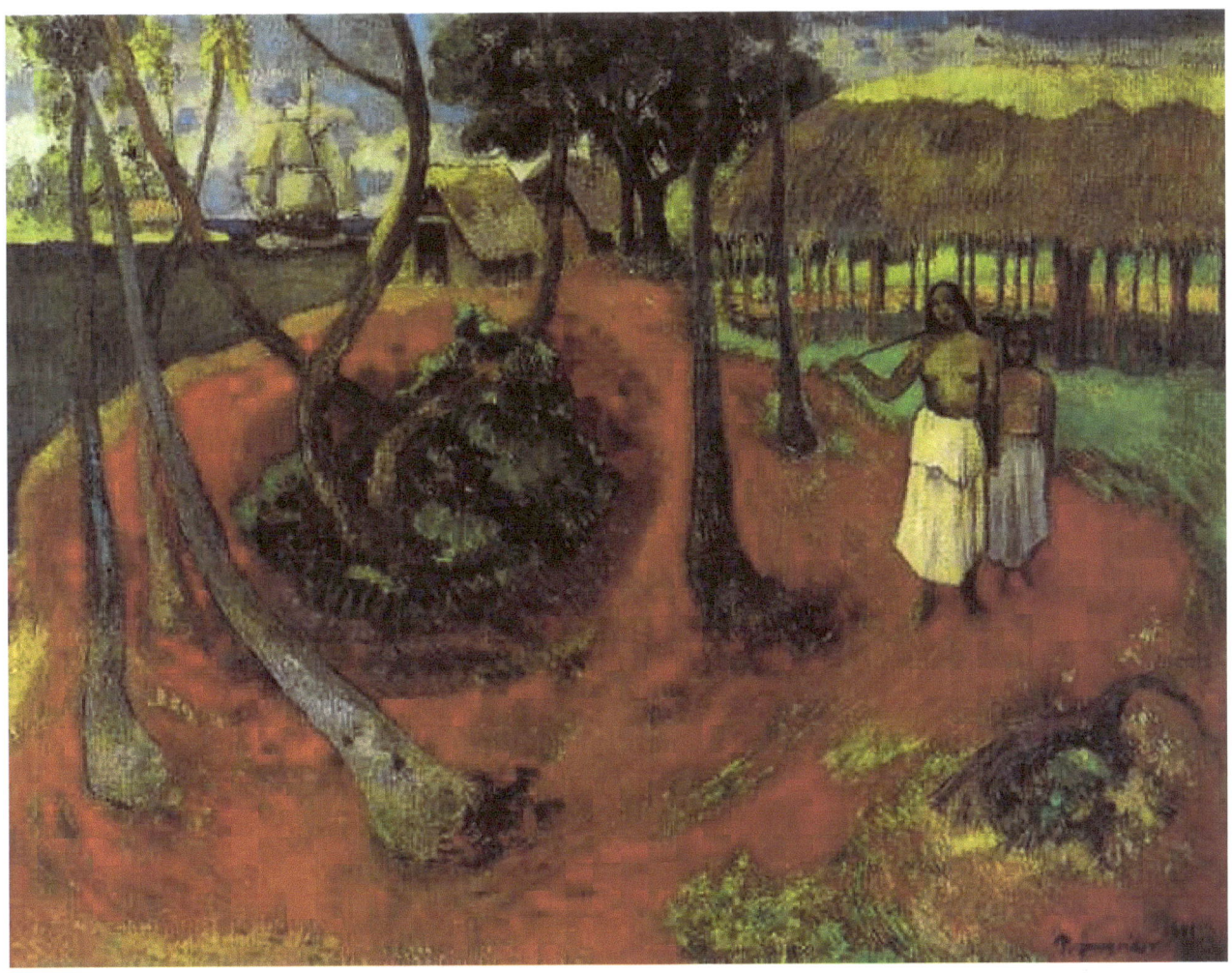

Tahitian idyll—1901--French Polynesia--Cloisonnism--2nd Tahiti period

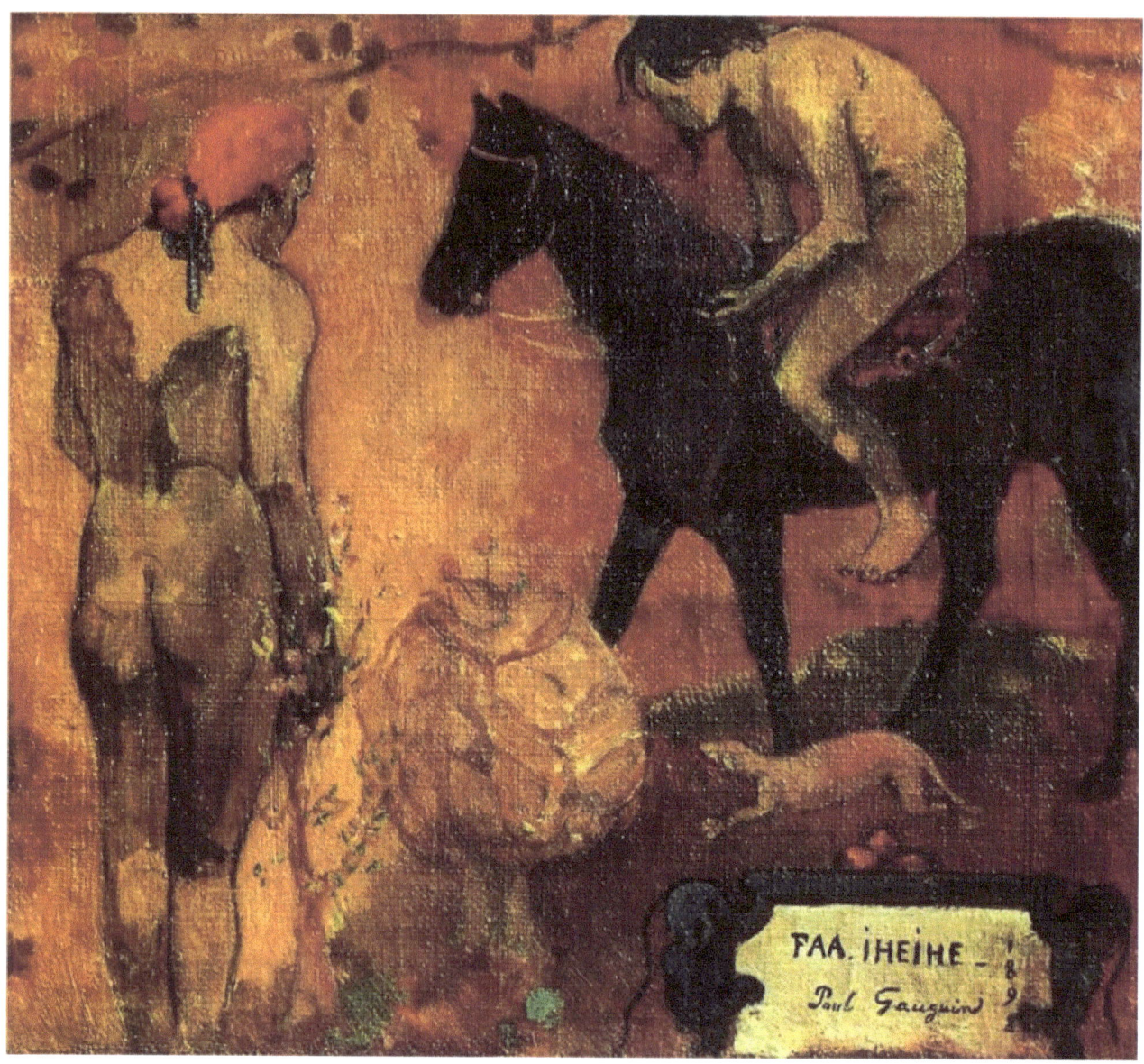

Tahitian pastoral—1892--French Polynesia--Post-Impressionism--1st Tahiti period

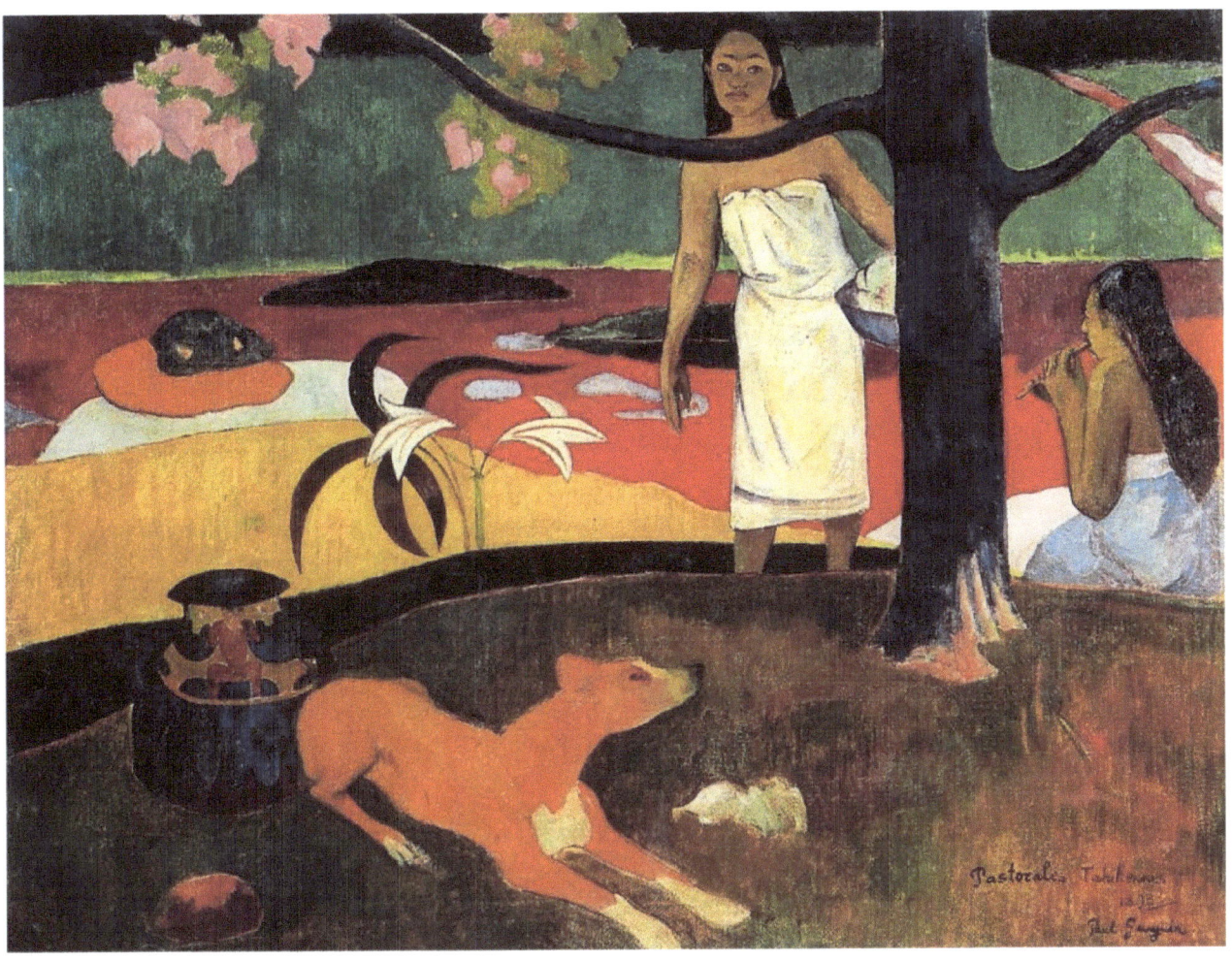

Tahitian pastorale—1898--Punaauia, French Polynesia--Post-Impressionism--2nd
Tahiti period

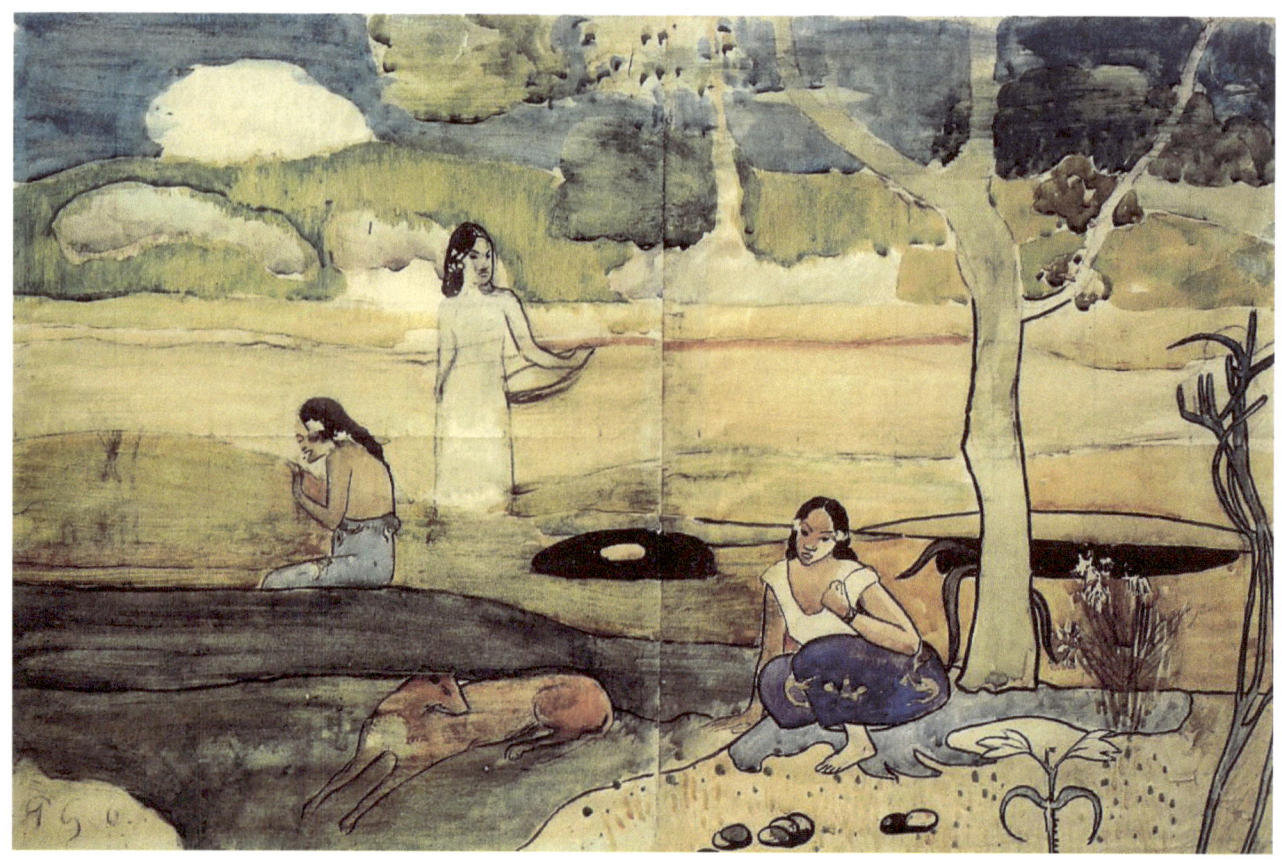

Tahitian Scene –1892--French Polynesia--Japonism--1st Tahiti period

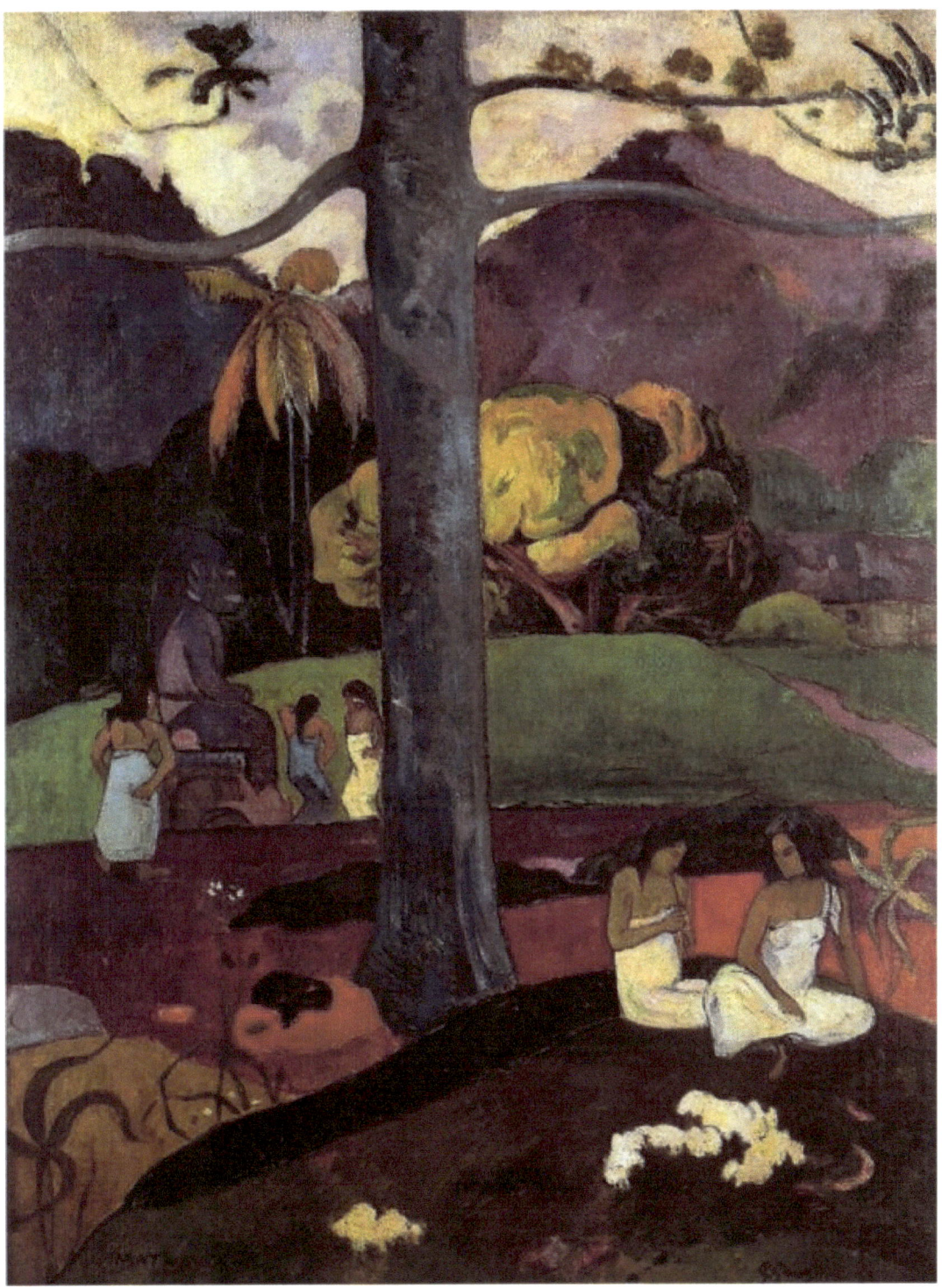

Olden times—1892--French Polynesia--Cloisonnism--1st Tahiti period

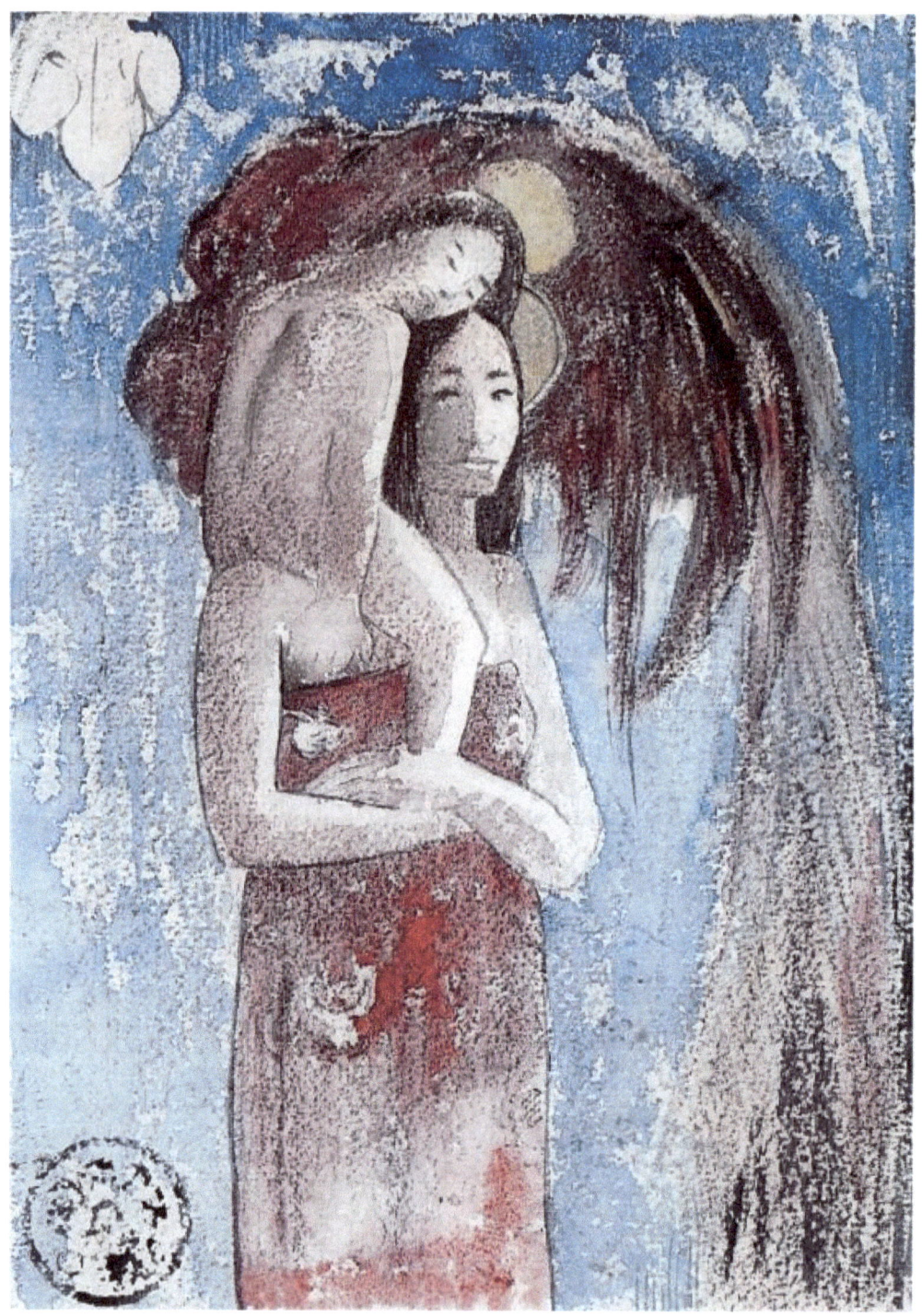

Orana Maria (Hail Maria)—1894--Paris, France--Post-Impressionism

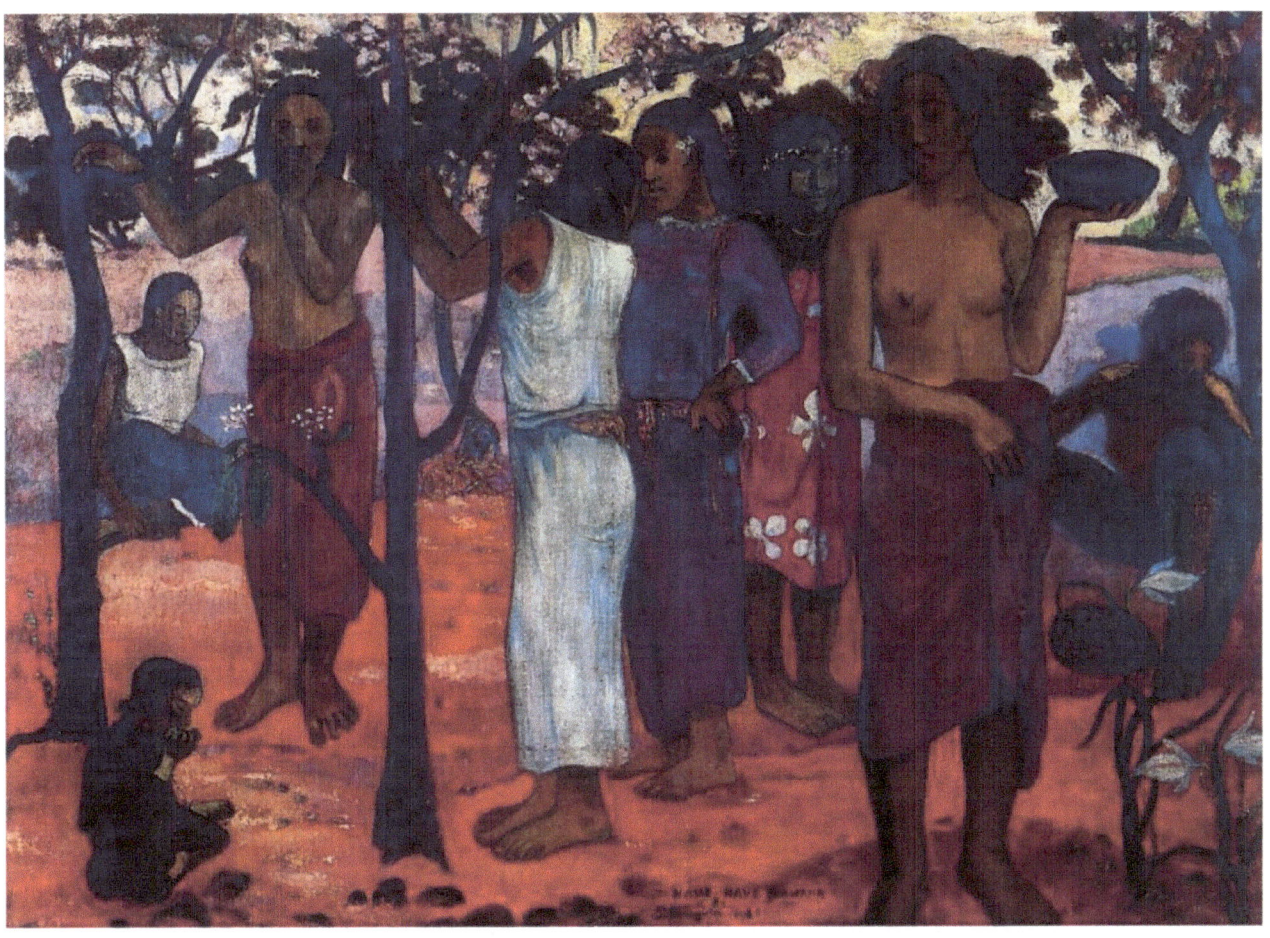

Perfect days—1896--French Polynesia--Post-Impressionism--2nd Tahiti period

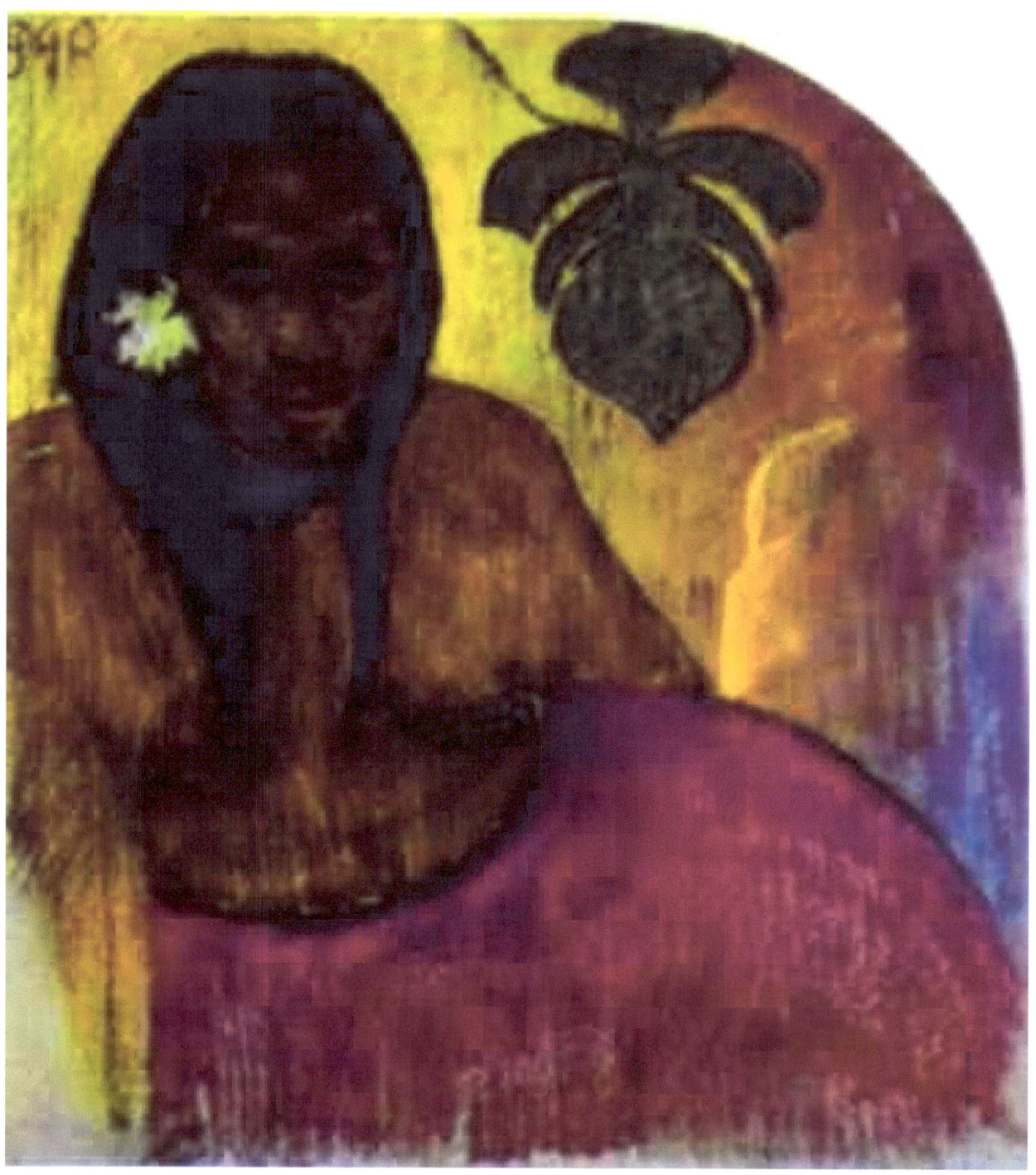

Tahitian Woman –1899--French Polynesia--Post-Impressionism--2nd Tahiti period

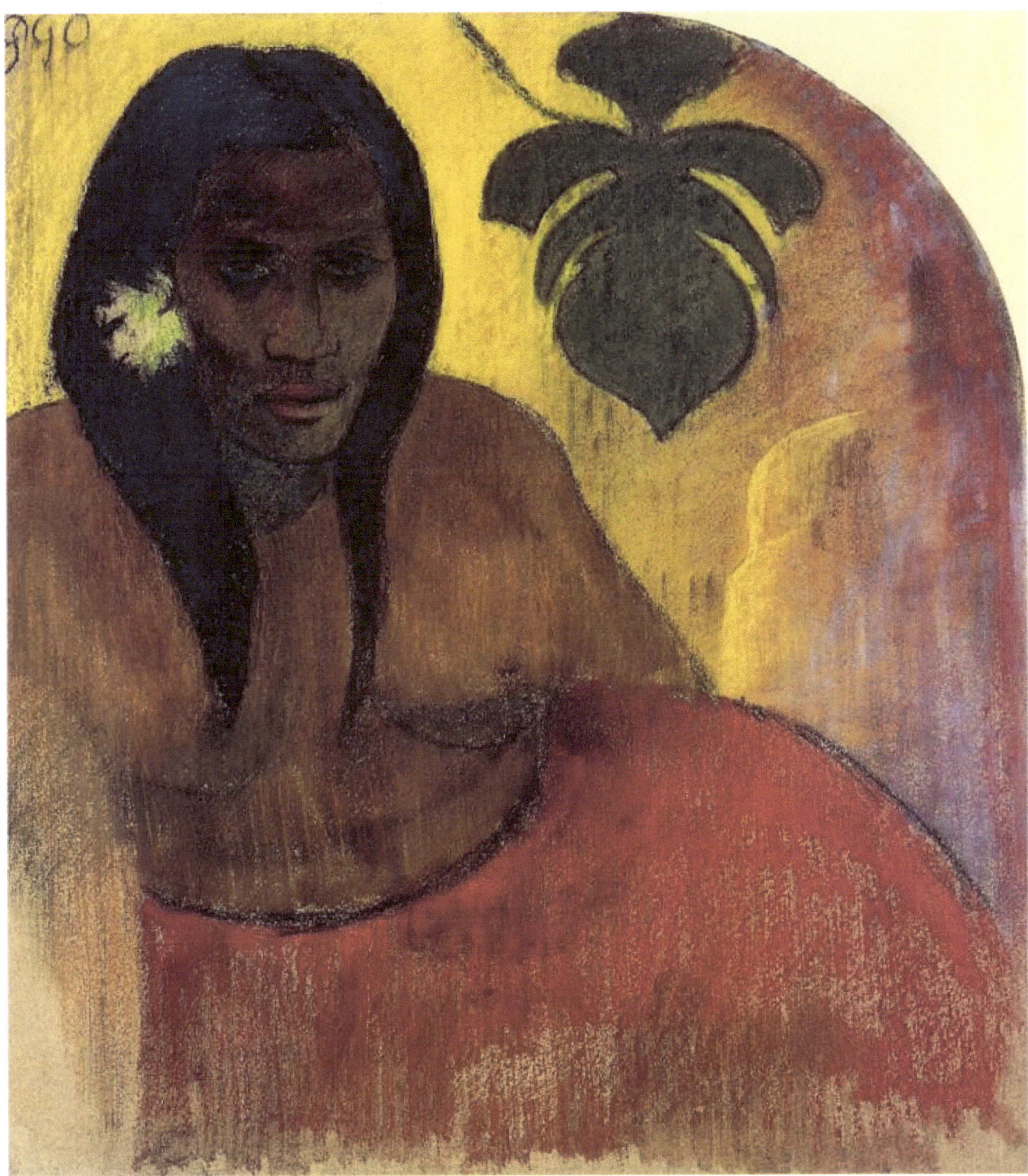

Tahitian Woman –1894--Post-Impressionism--Paris period

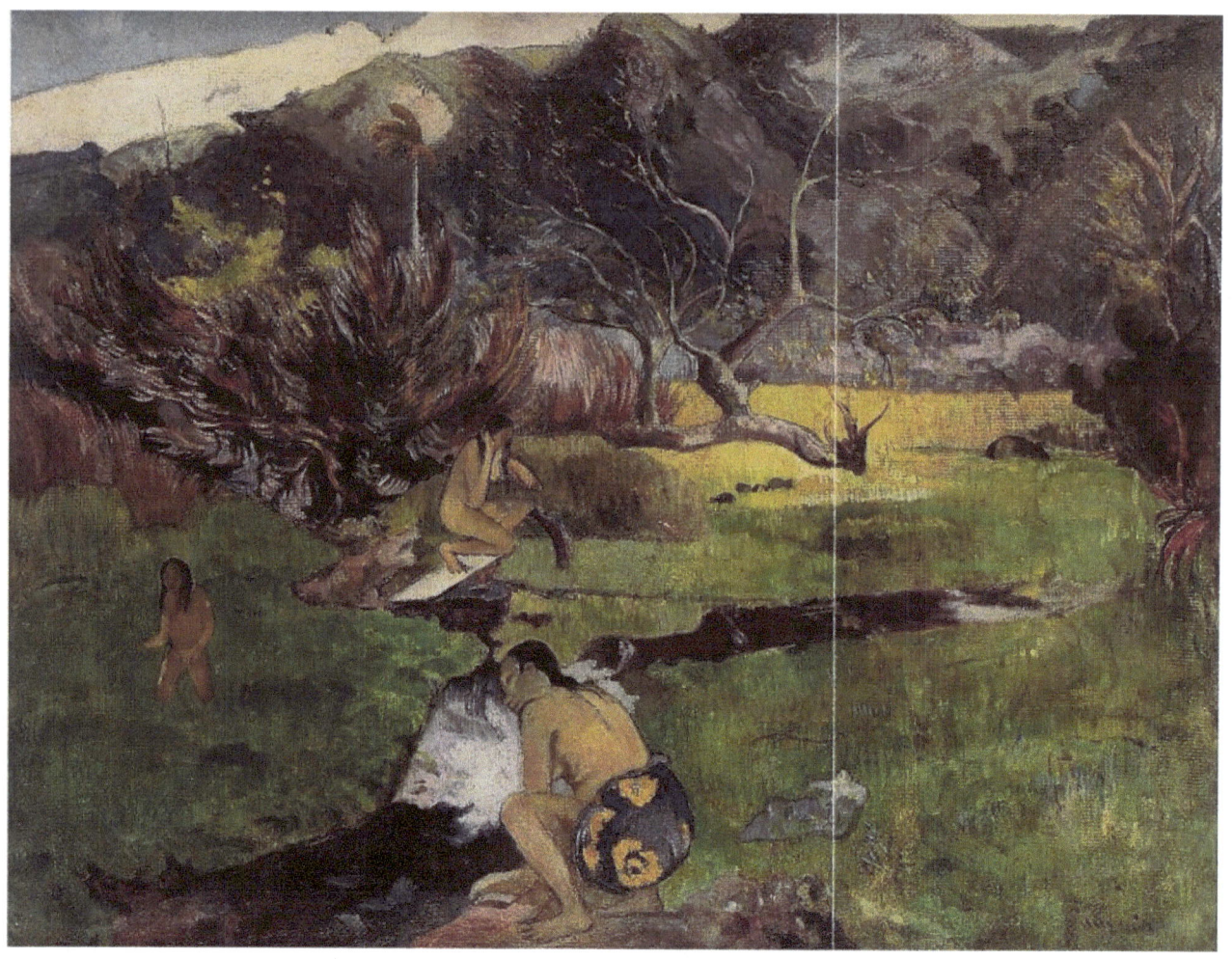

Tahitian woman near river--Artist: Paul Gauguin--French Polynesia--Cloisonnism--1st Tahiti period

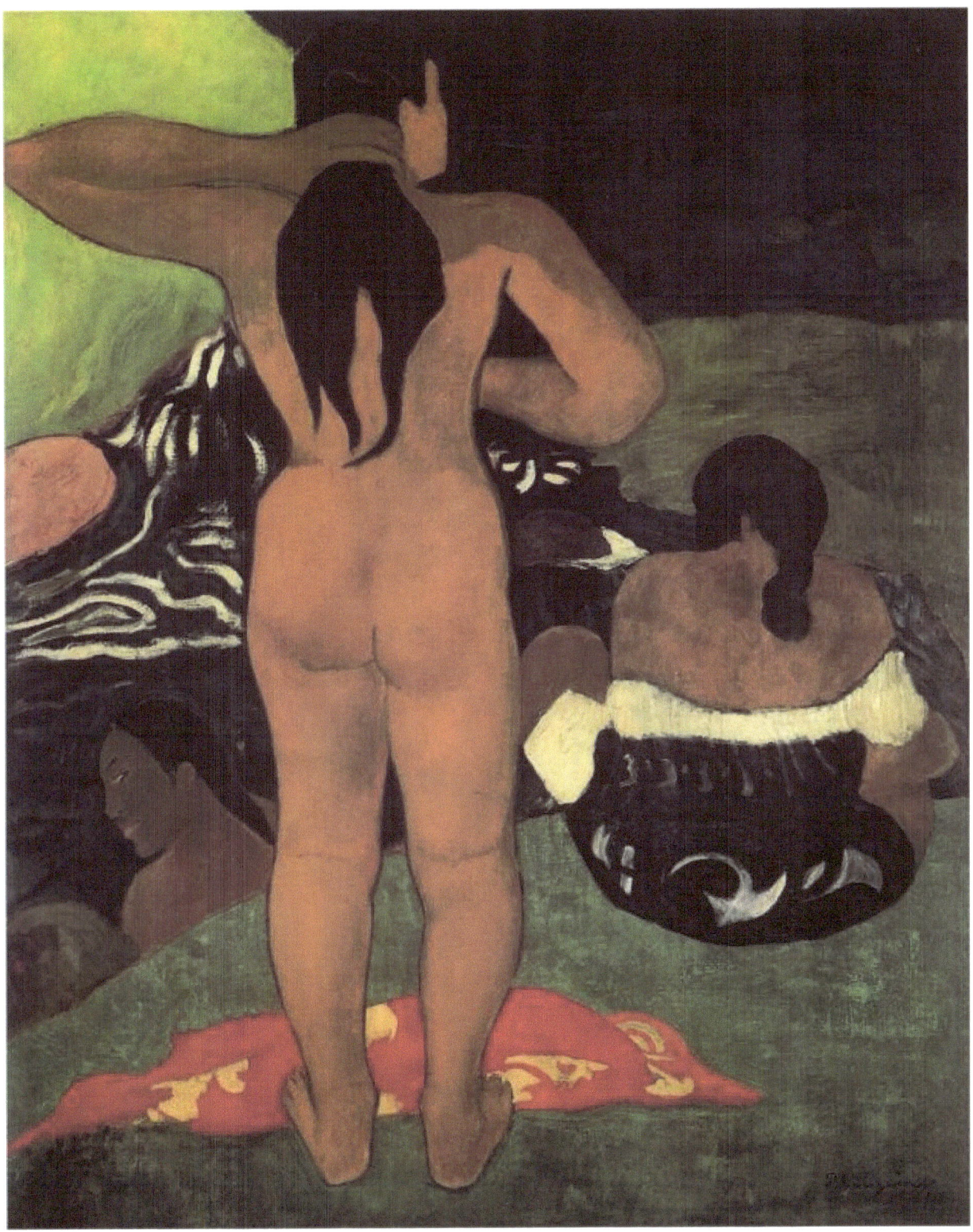

Tahitian women on the beach—1892--French Polynesia--Cloisonnism--

1st Tahiti period

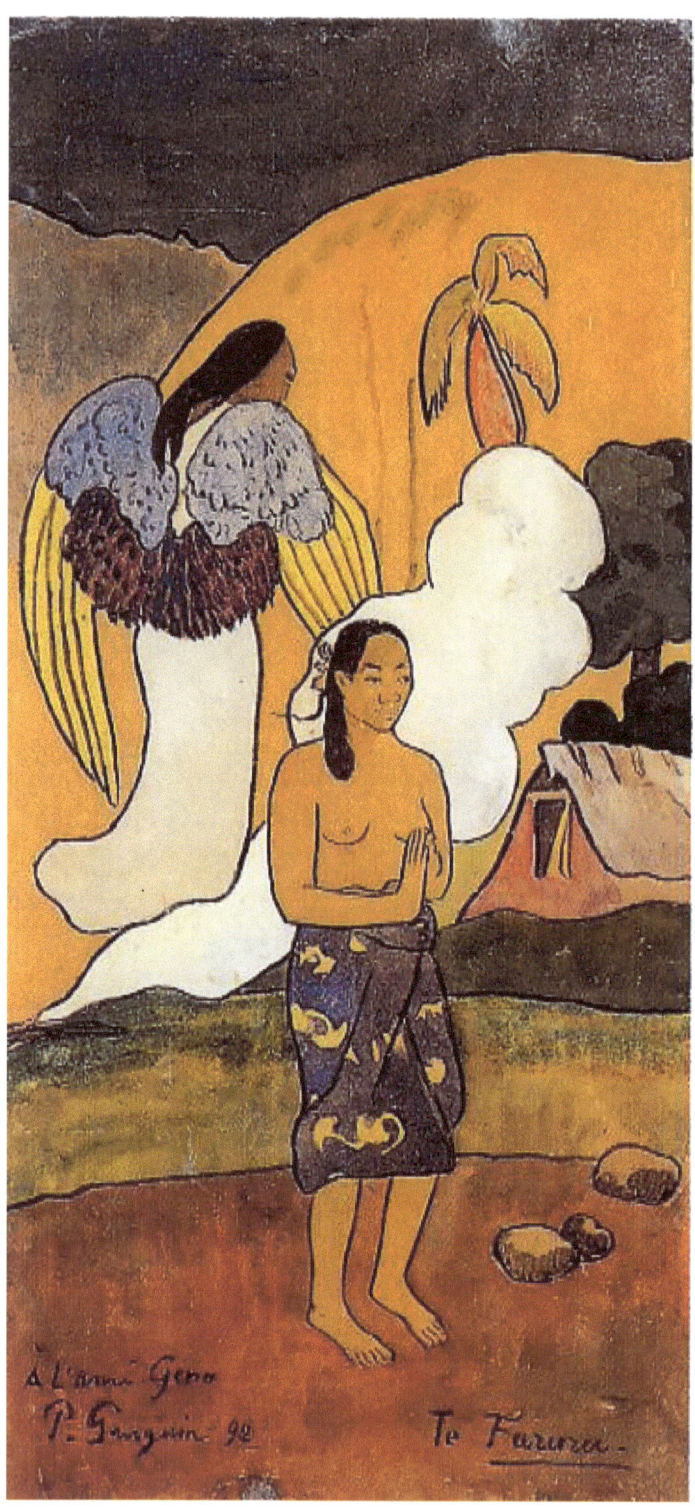

The encounter --Artist: Paul Gauguin--Completion Date: 1892--French Polynesia--Cloisonnism--1st Tahiti period

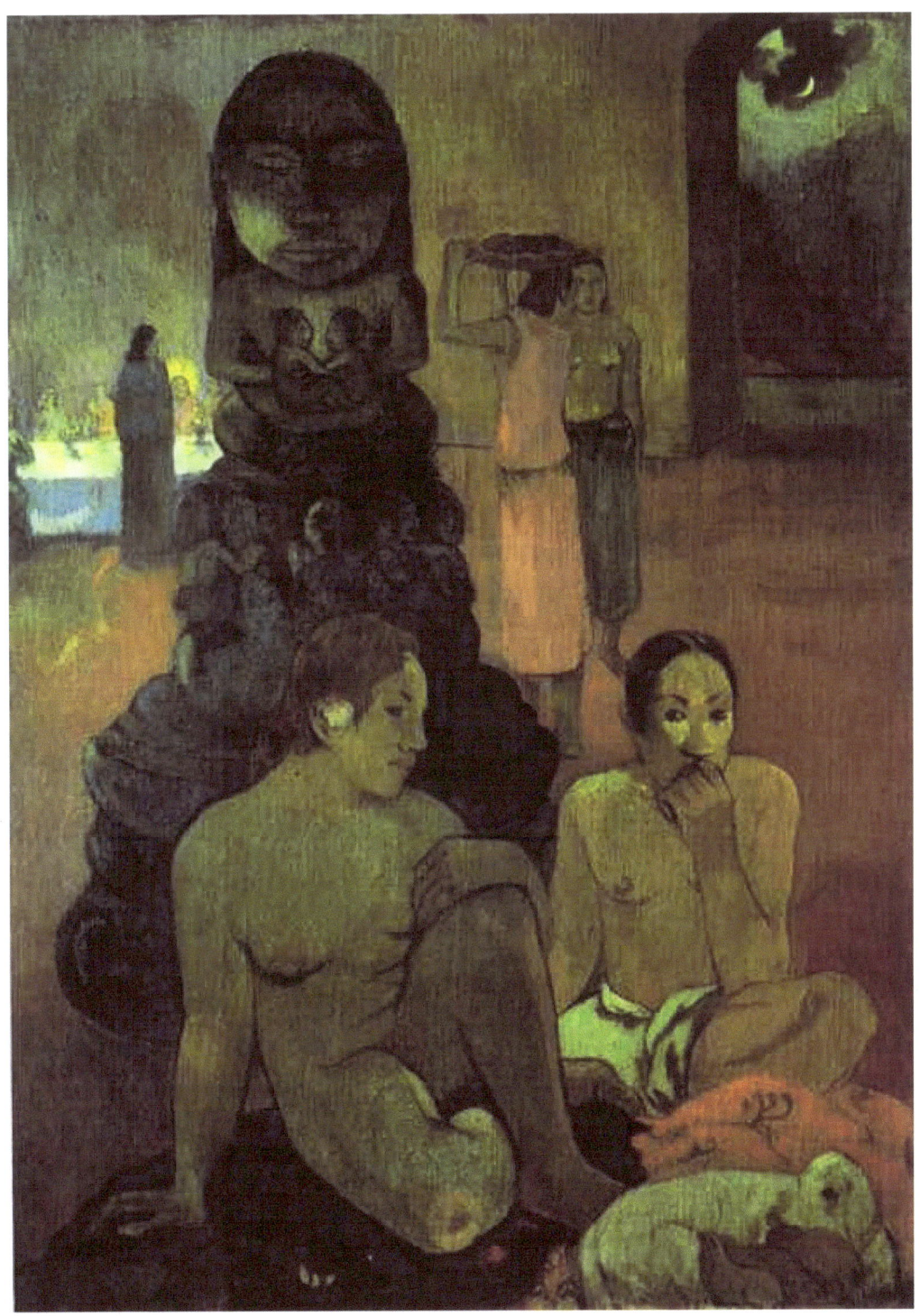

The Great Buddha—1899--Punaauia, French Polynesia--Post-Impressionism--
2nd Tahiti period

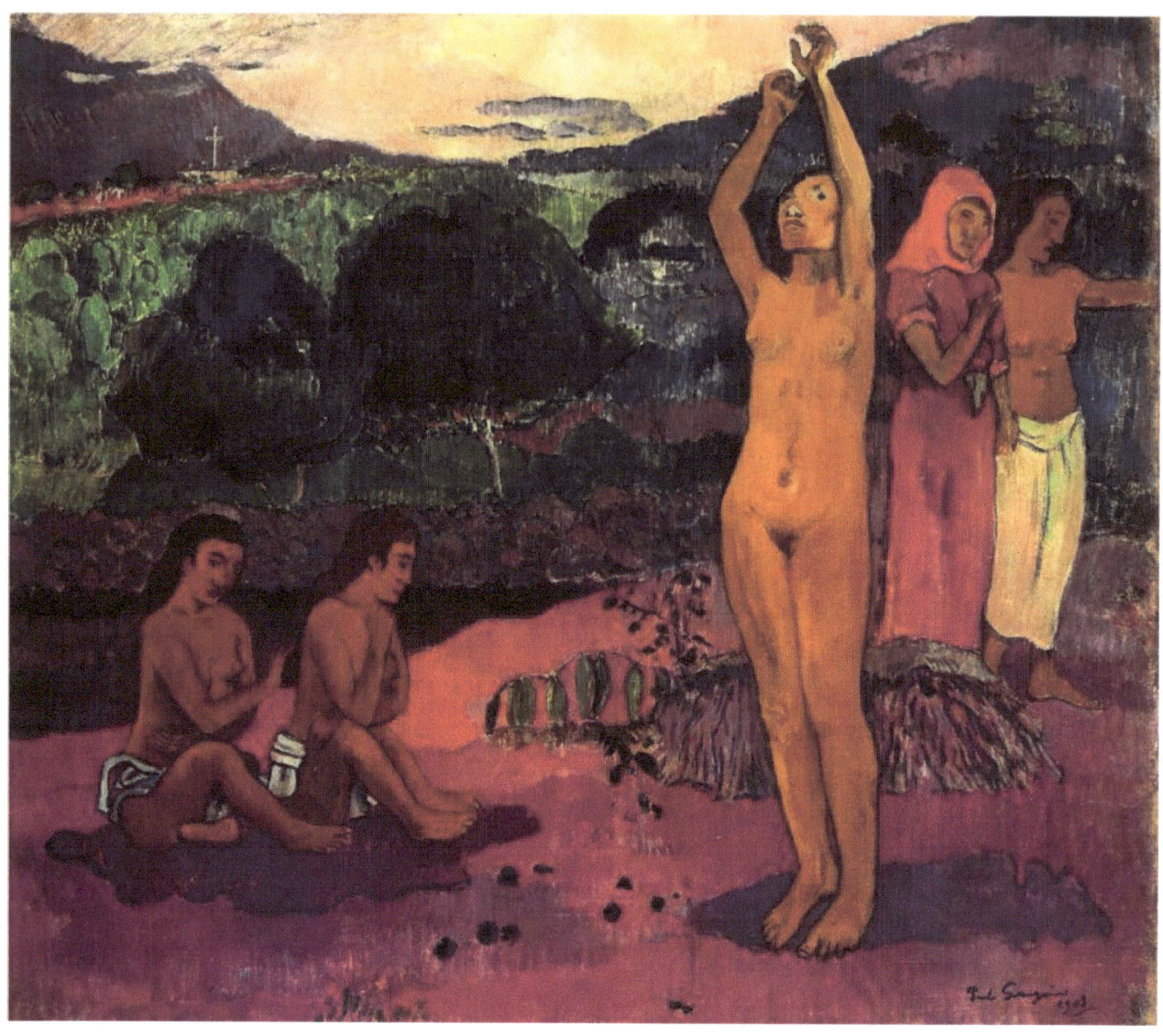

The Invocation—1903--French Polynesia--Post-Impressionism--2nd Tahiti period

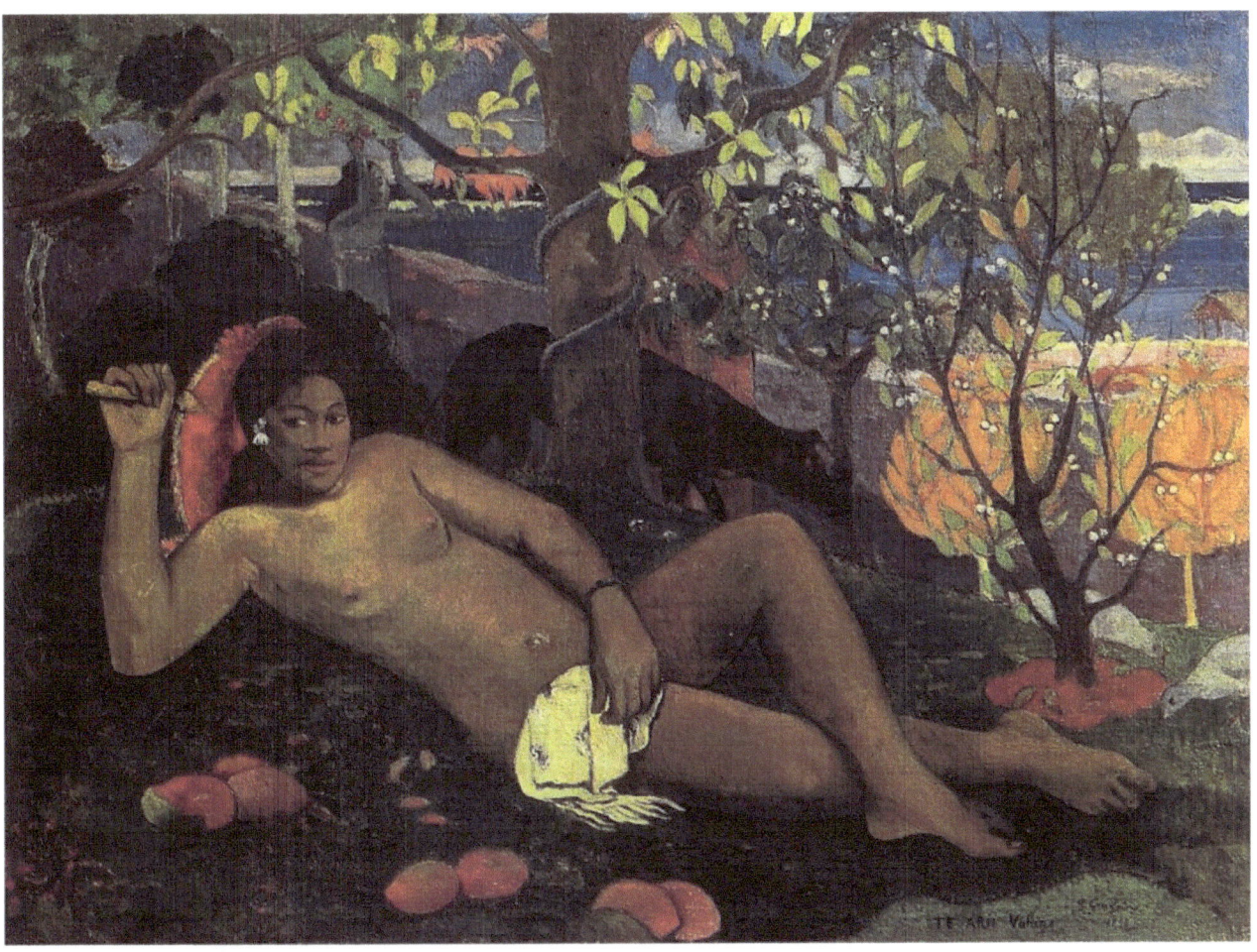

The King's Wife—1896--French Polynesia--Cloisonnism--2nd Tahiti period

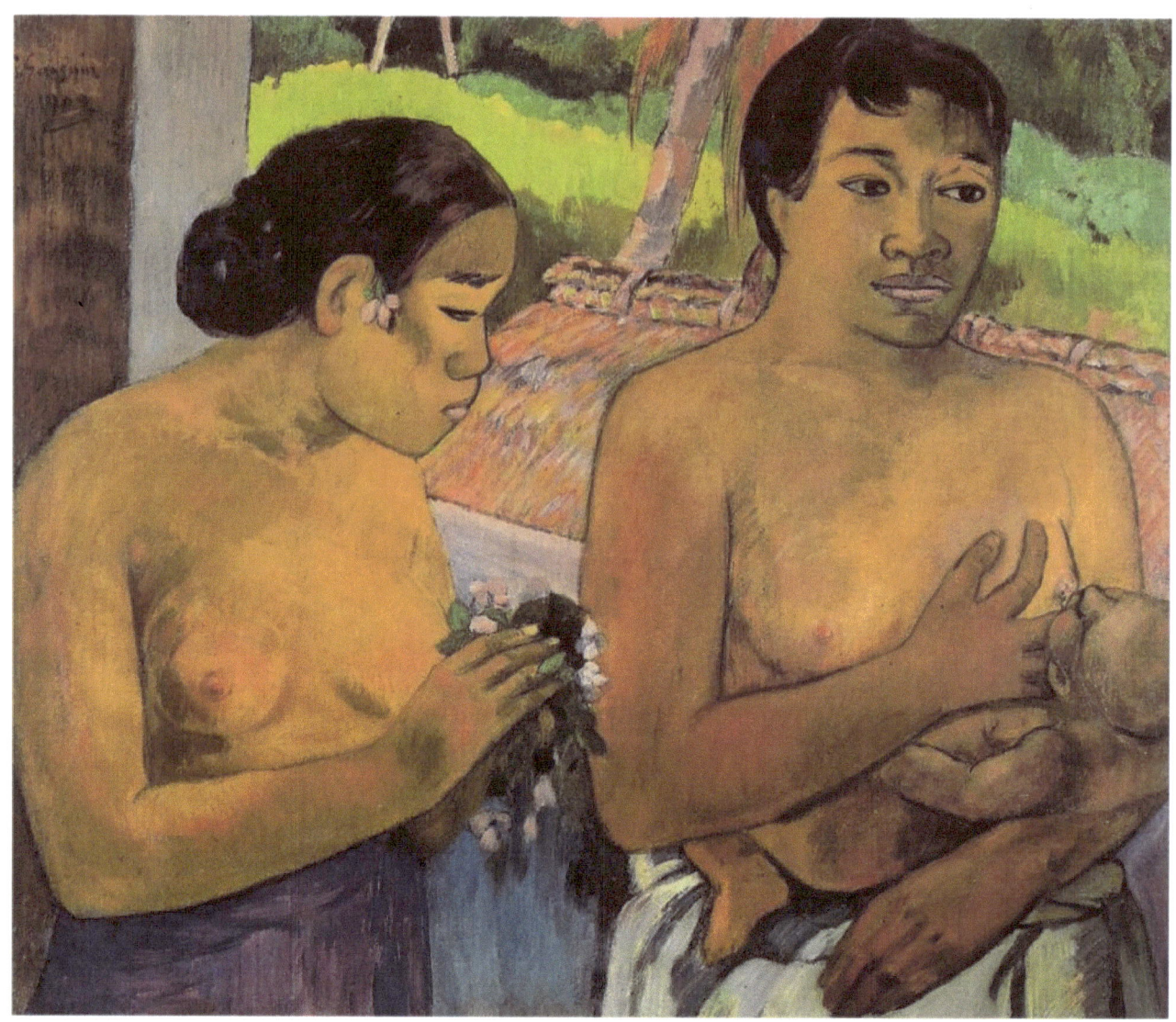

The Offering—1902--French Polynesia--Cloisonnism--2nd Tahiti period

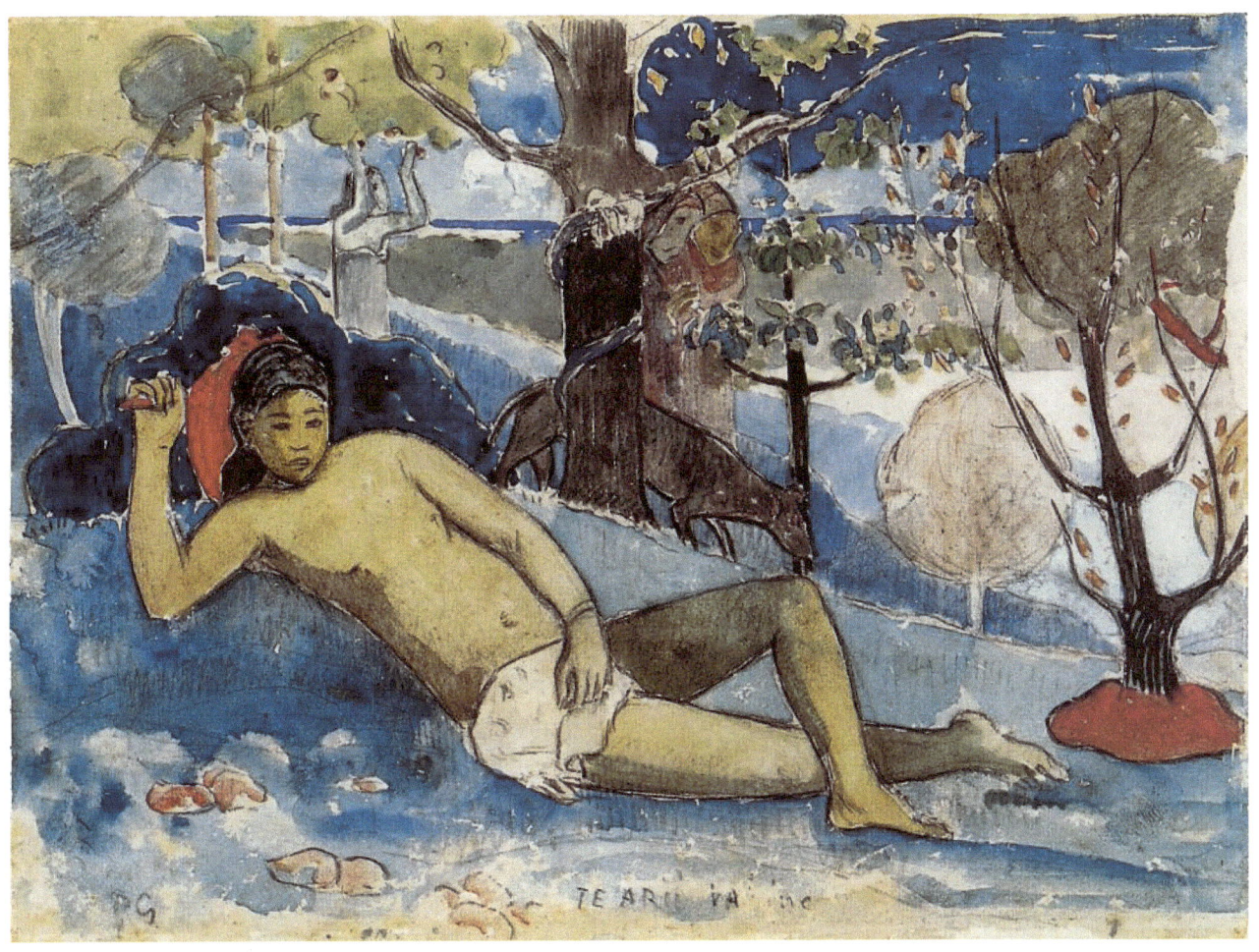

The queen of beauty –1896--Place of Creation: French Polynesia--Post-Impressionism--2nd Tahiti period

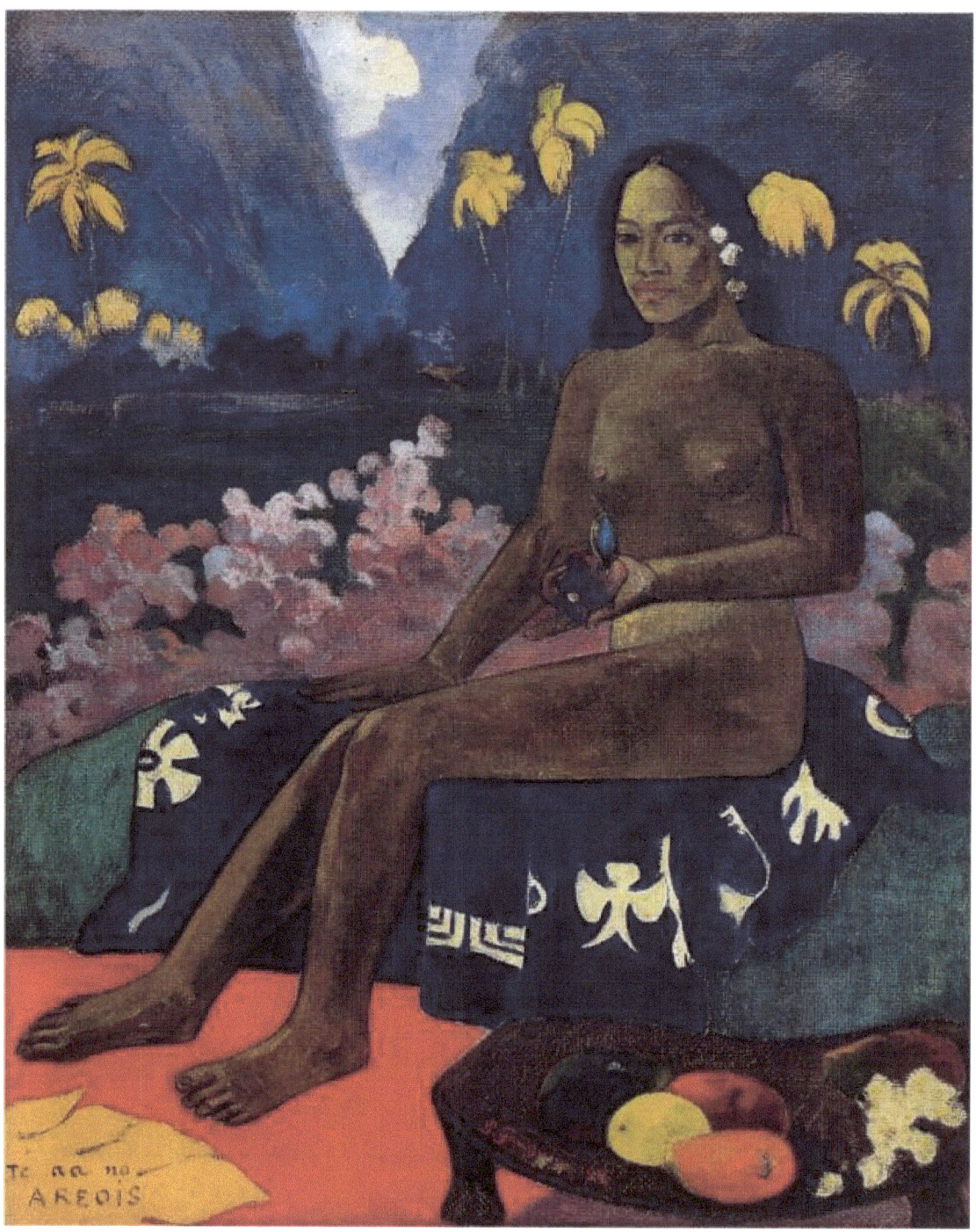

The Seed of the Areoi—1892--French Polynesia--Post-Impressionism--1st Tahiti period

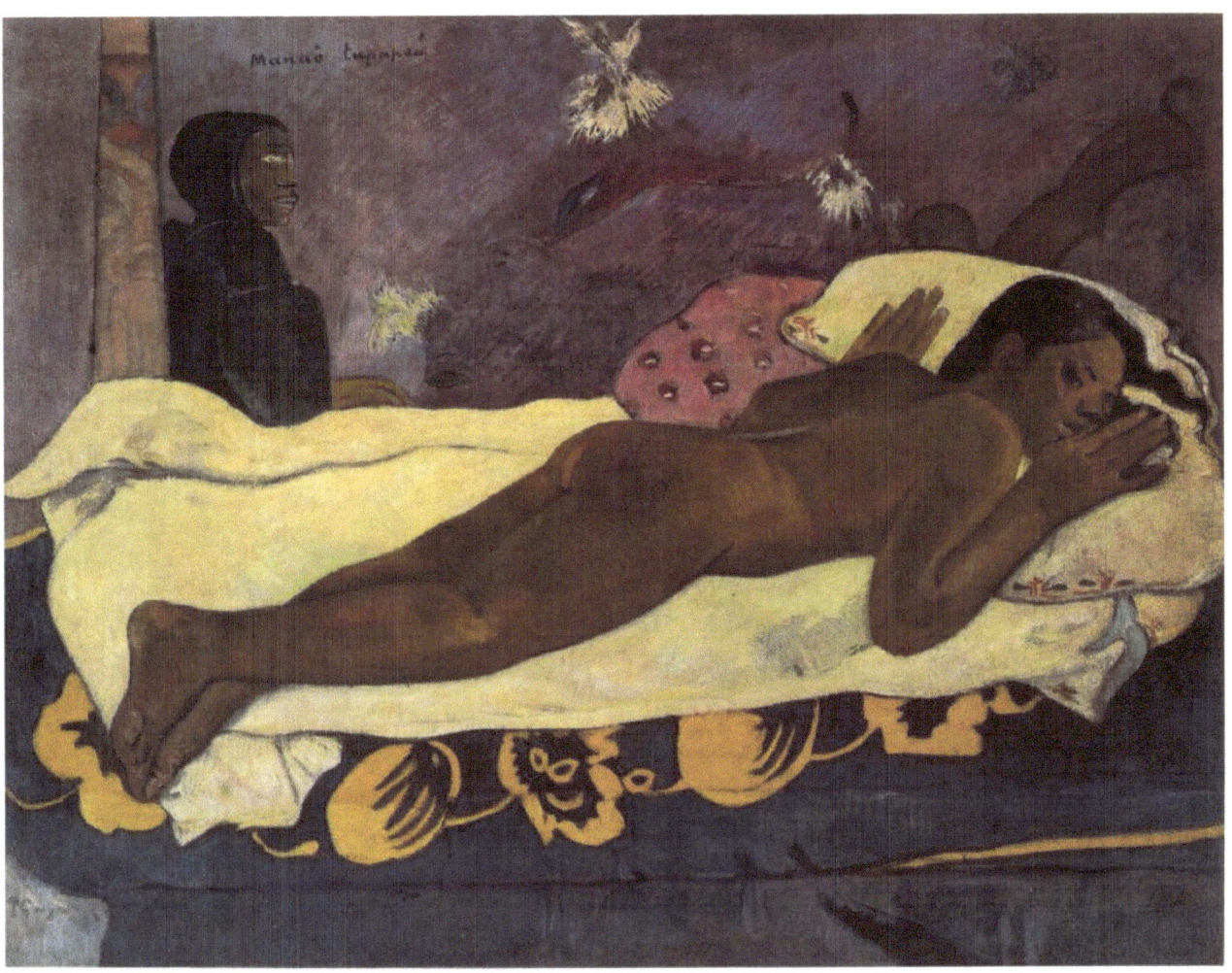

Spirit of the Dead Watching—1892--French Polynesia--Post-Impressionism--
1st Tahiti period

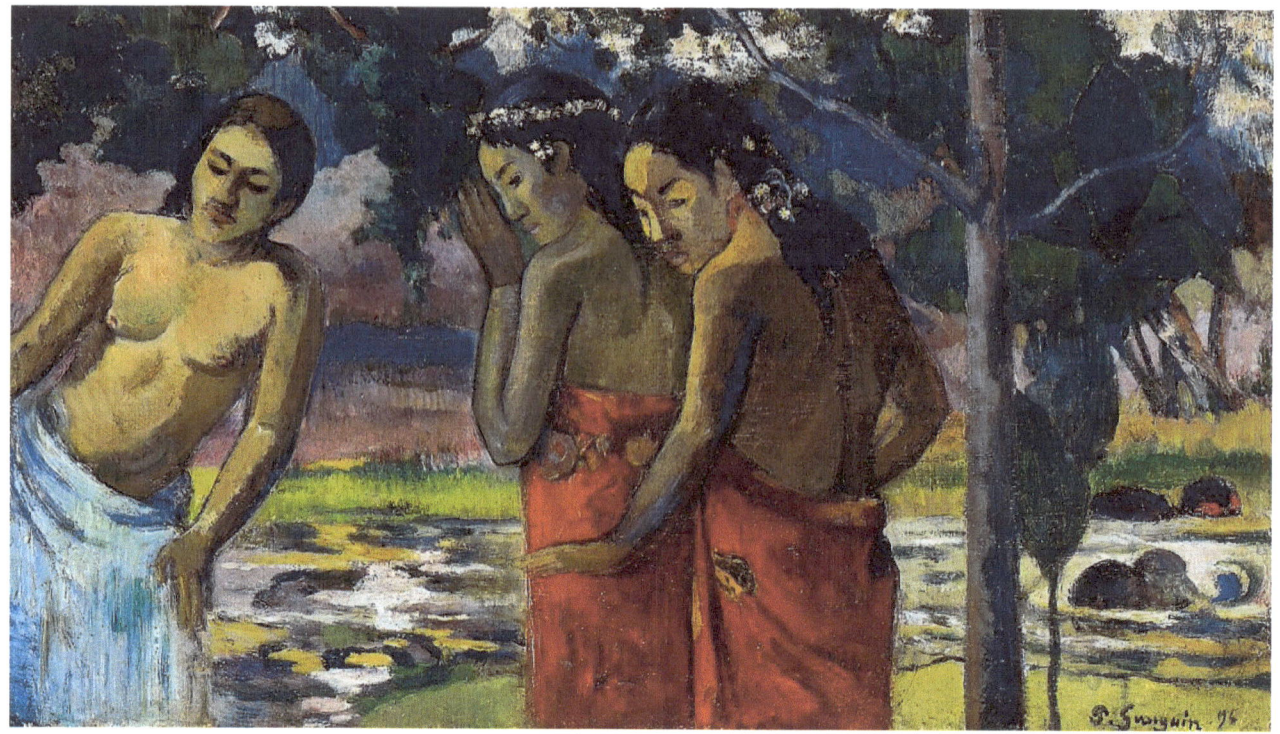

Three Tahitian Women—1896--French Polynes--Post-Impressionism--2nd Tahiti period

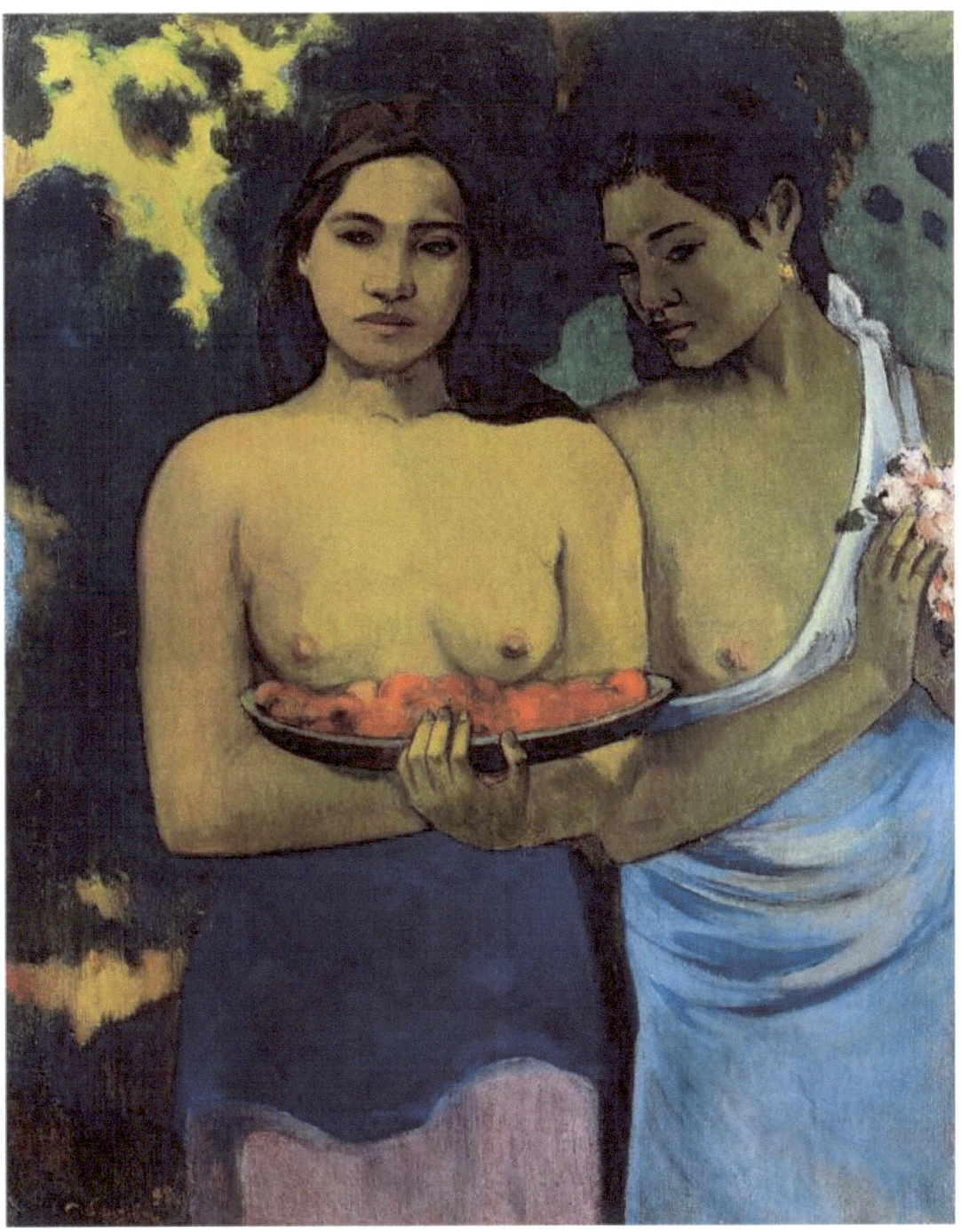

Two tahitian women—1899--Punaauia, French Polynesia--Cloisonnism

2nd Tahiti period

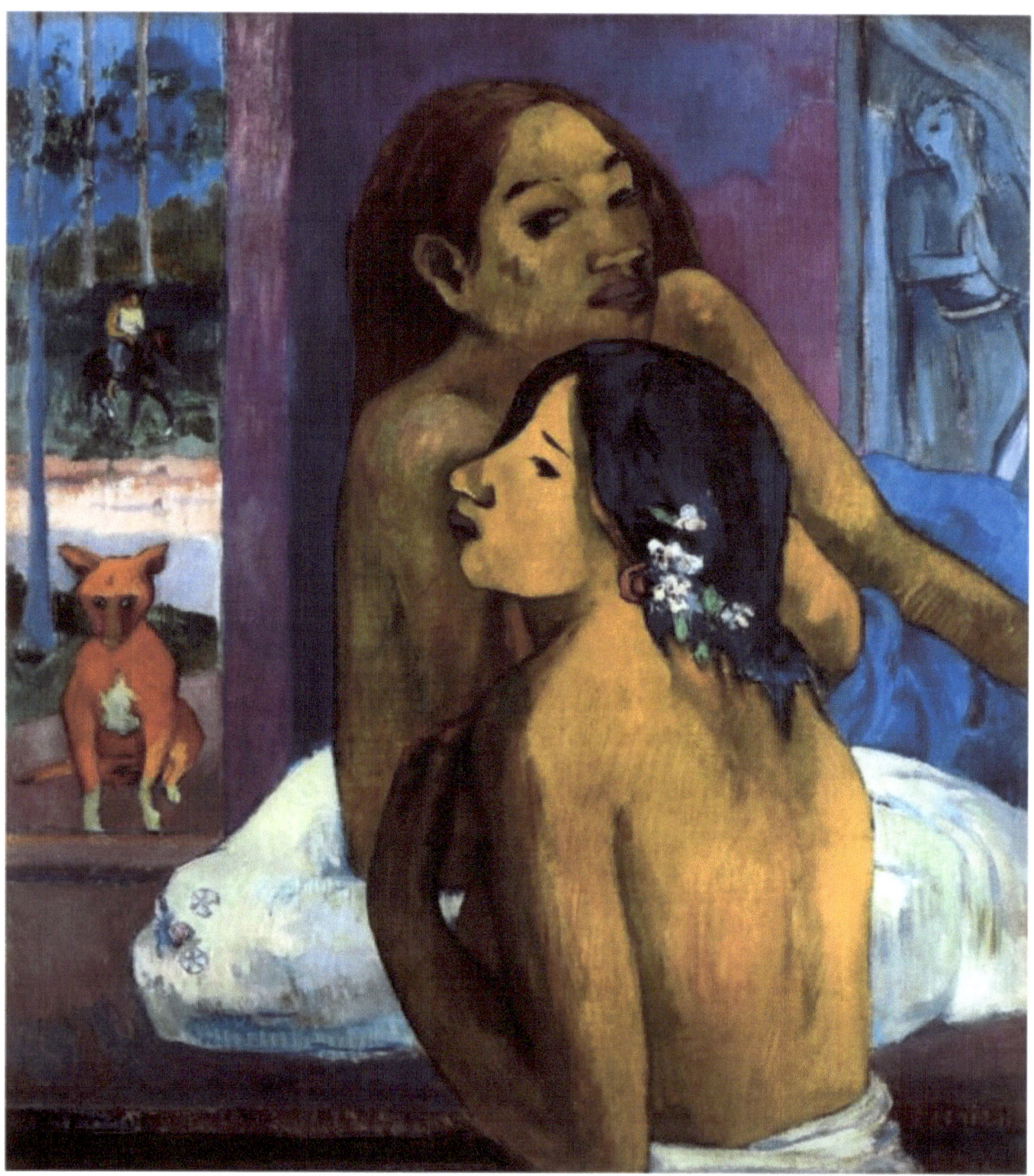

Two women (Flowered hair)—1902--French Polynesia--Cloisonnism--2nd Tahiti period

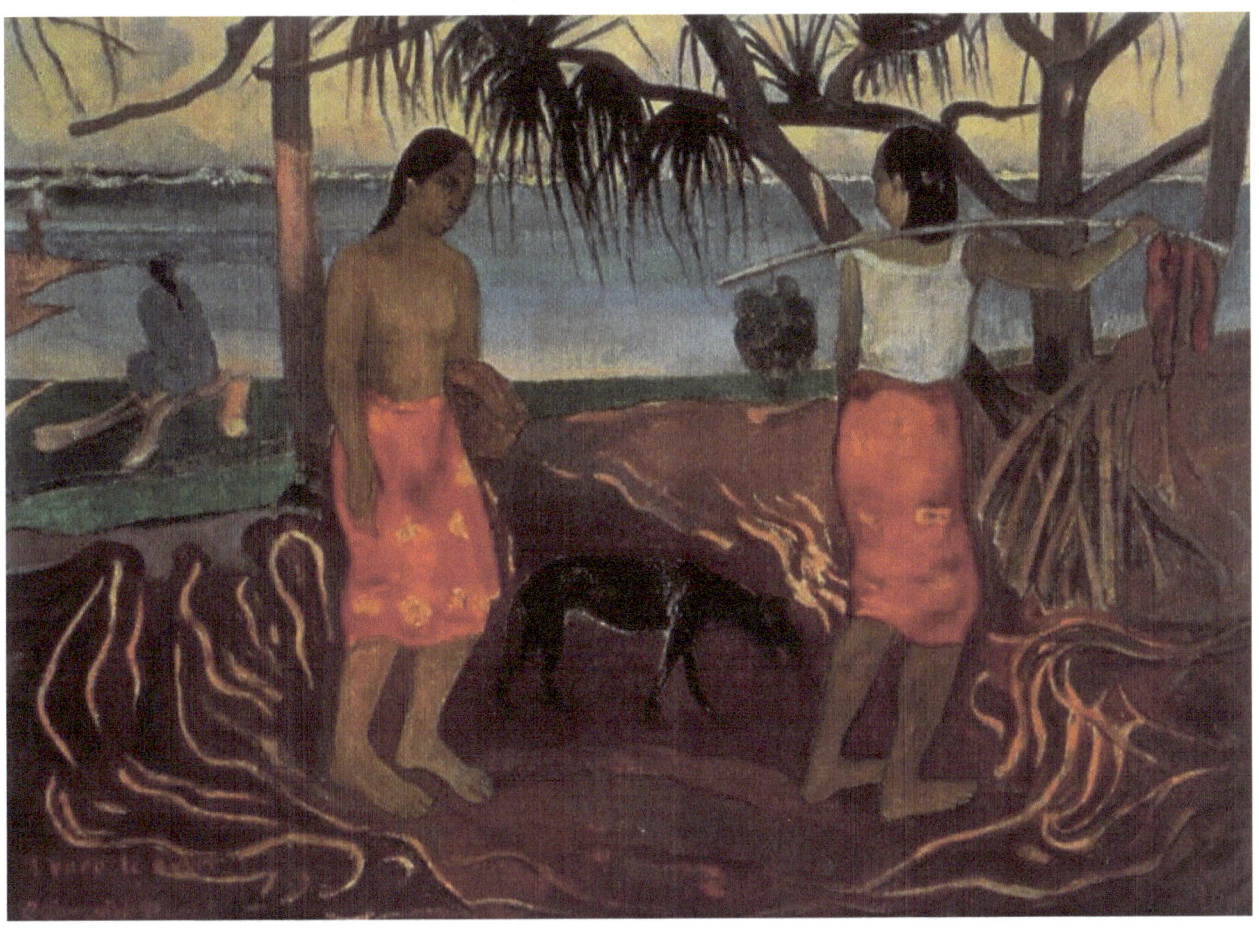

Under the Pandanus—189--French Polynesia--Cloisonnism--1st Tahiti period

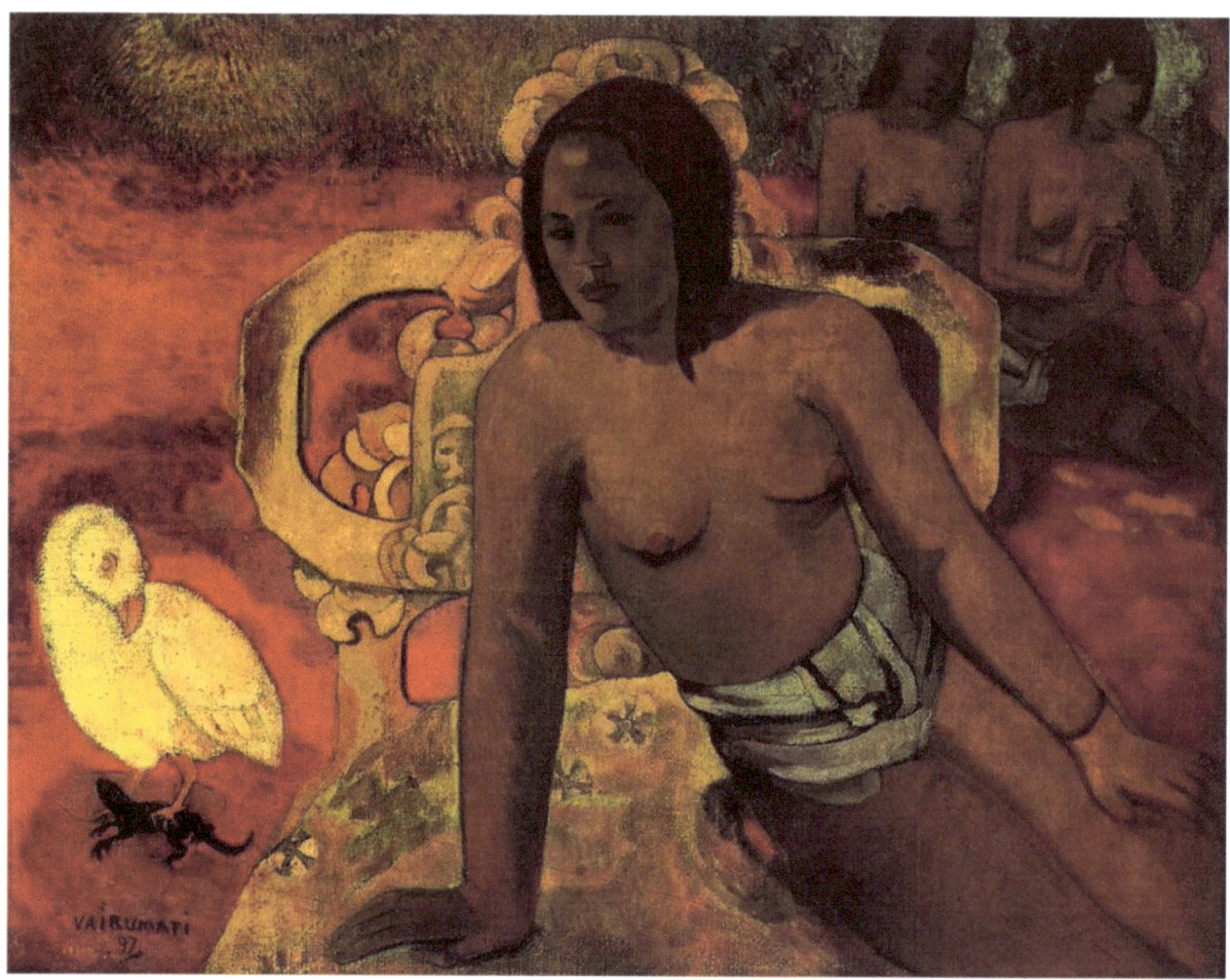

Vairumat—1892--French Polynesia--Post-Impressionism--1st Tahiti period

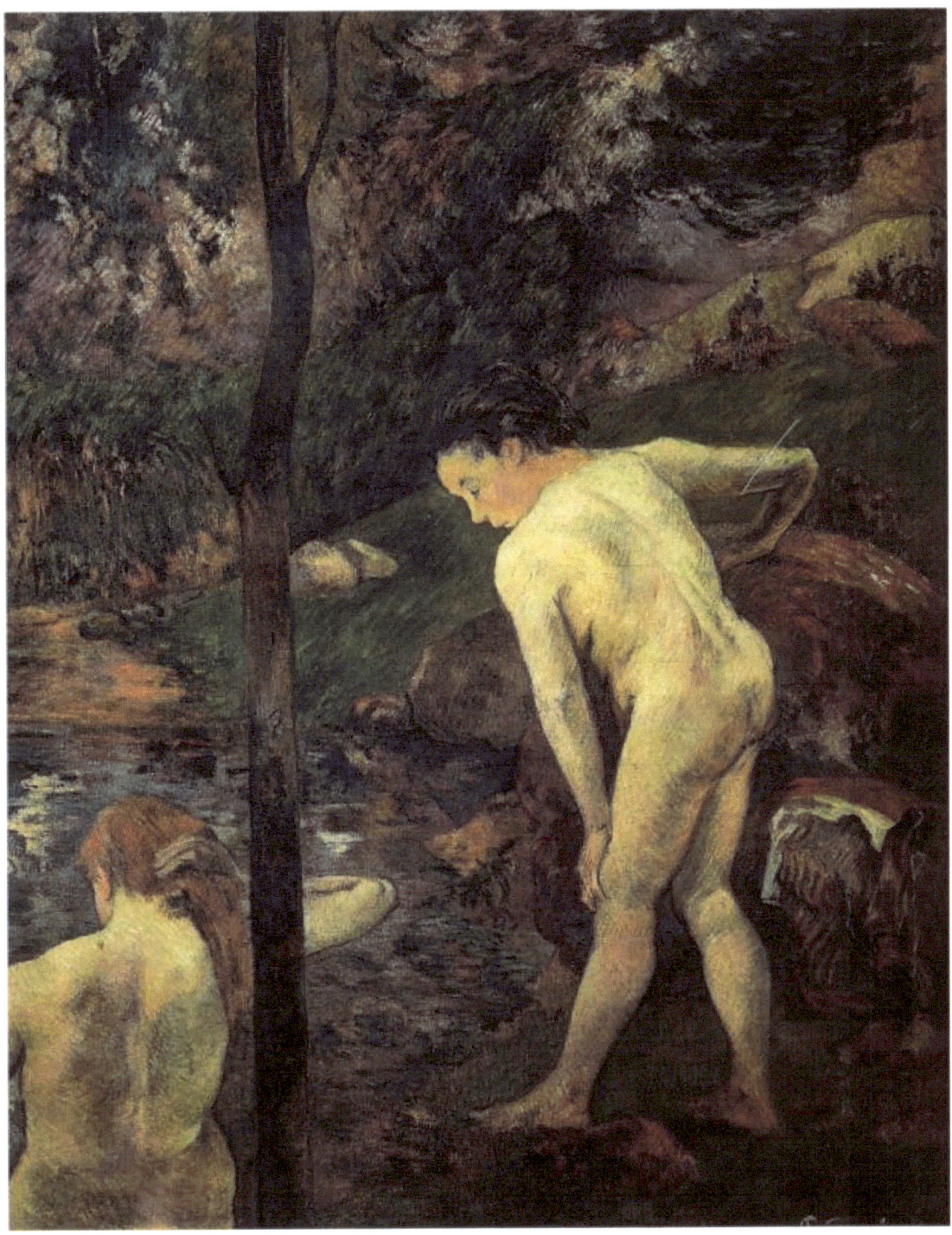

Two girls bathing –1887—France--Post-Impressionism

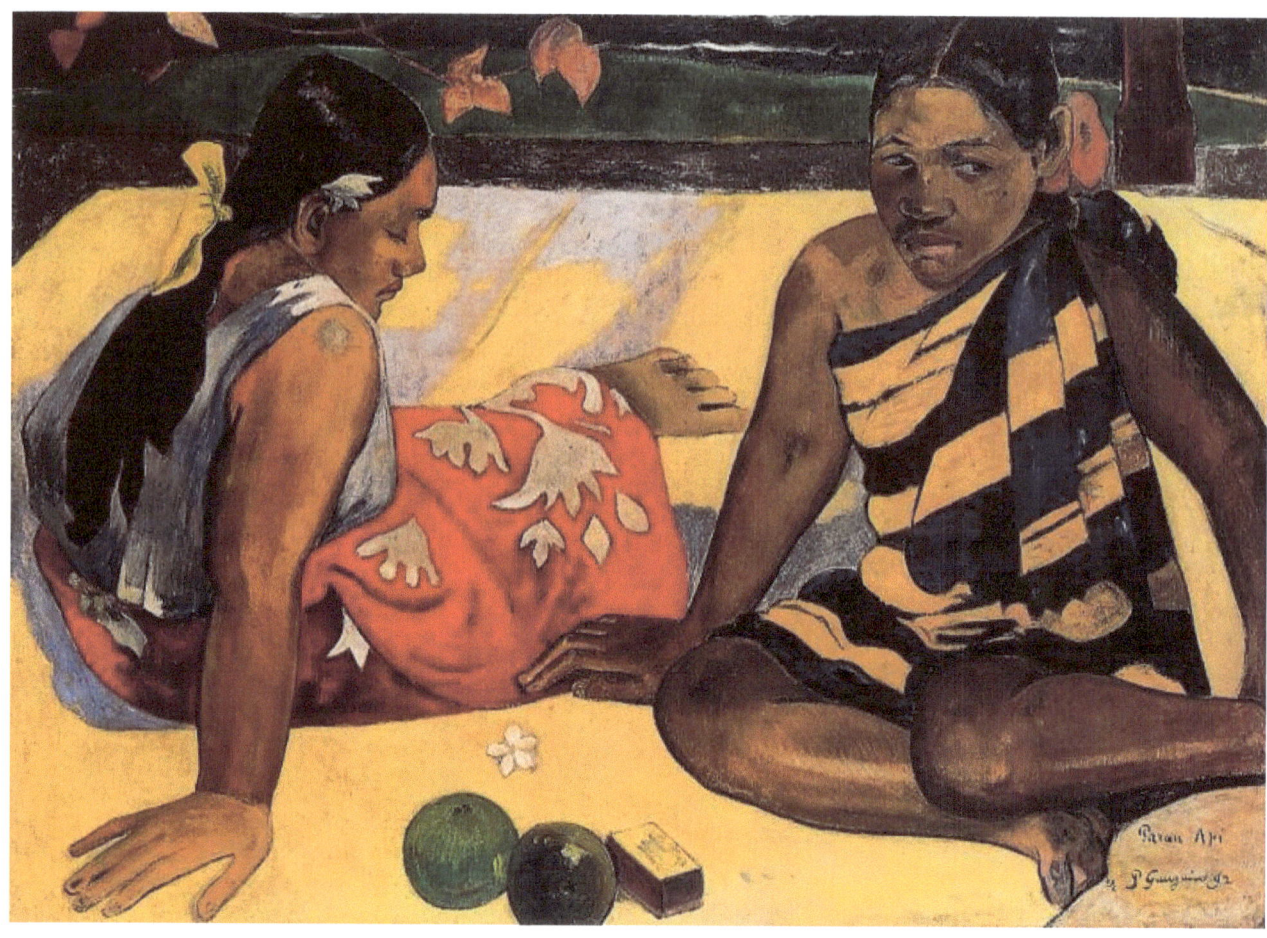

What's New? –1892--French Polynesia--Post-Impressionism--
1st Tahiti period

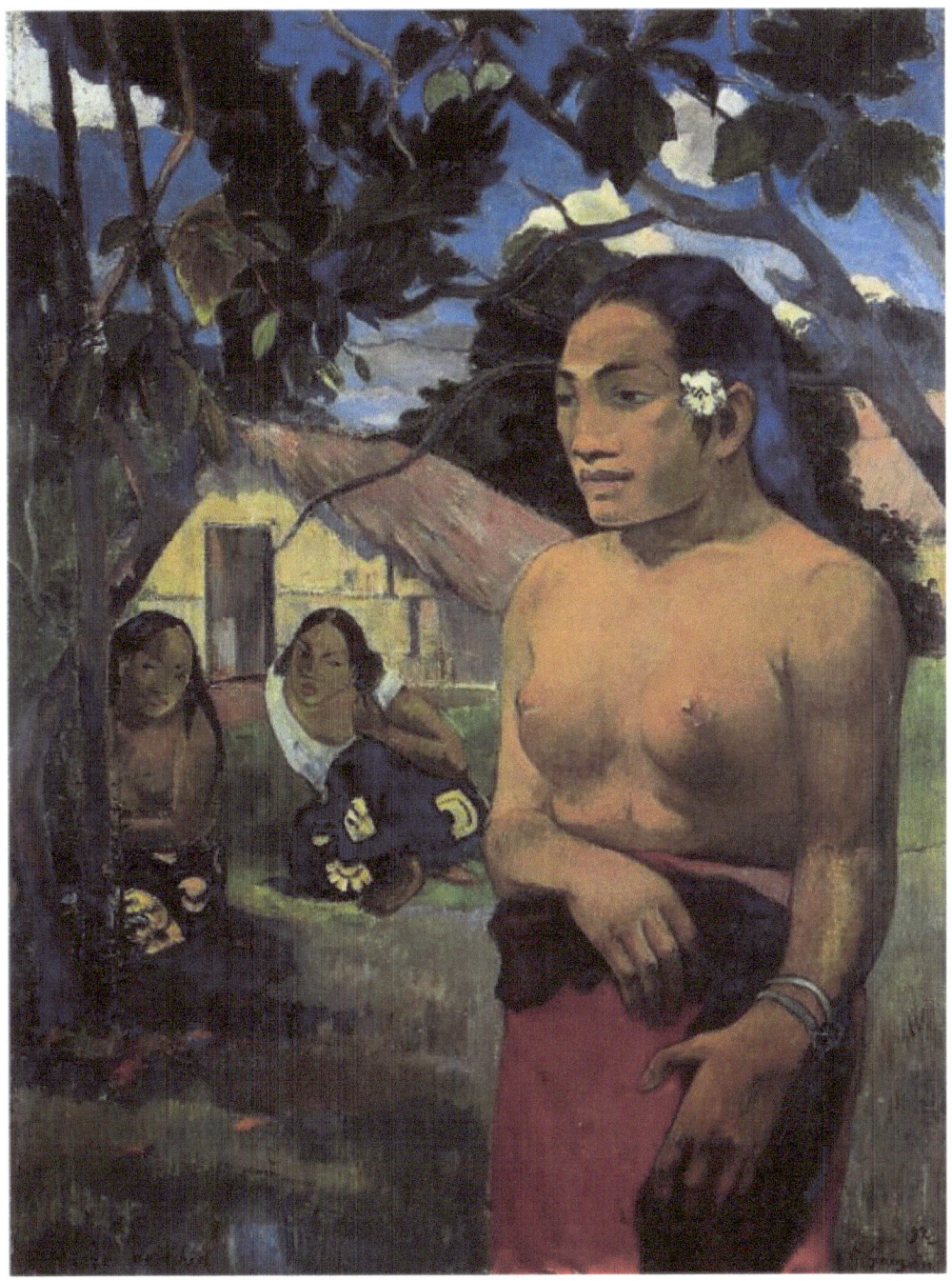

Where are you going?——1892--French Polynesia--Cloisonnism--1st Tahiti period

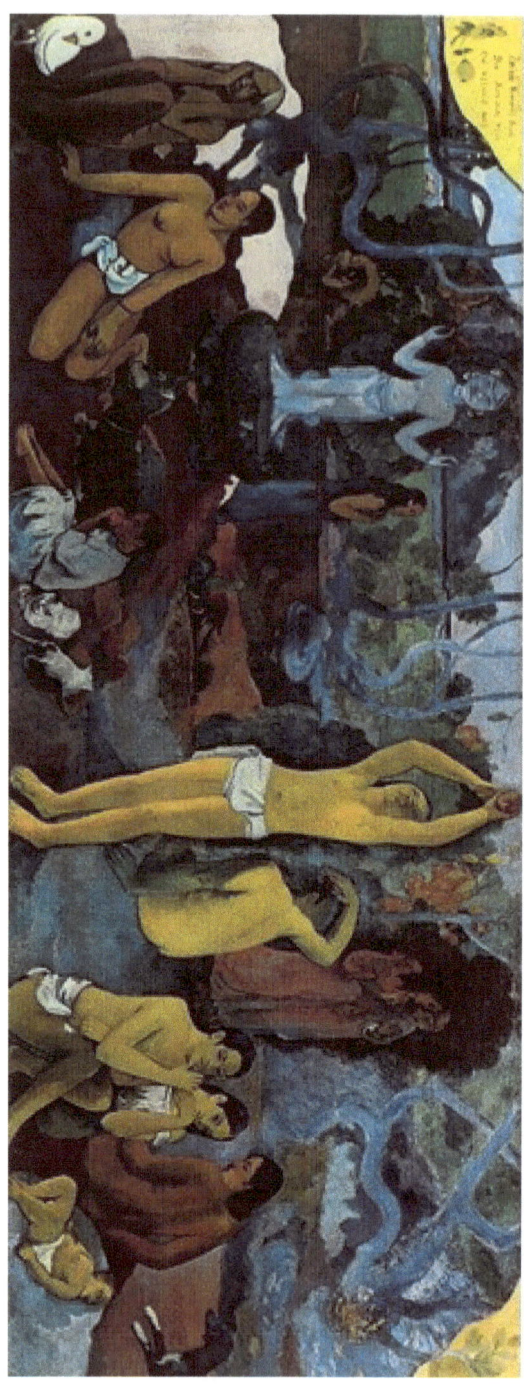

Where Do We Come From? What Are We? Where Are We Going?——1897--Punaauia, French Polynesia--Post-Impressionism--2nd Tahiti period

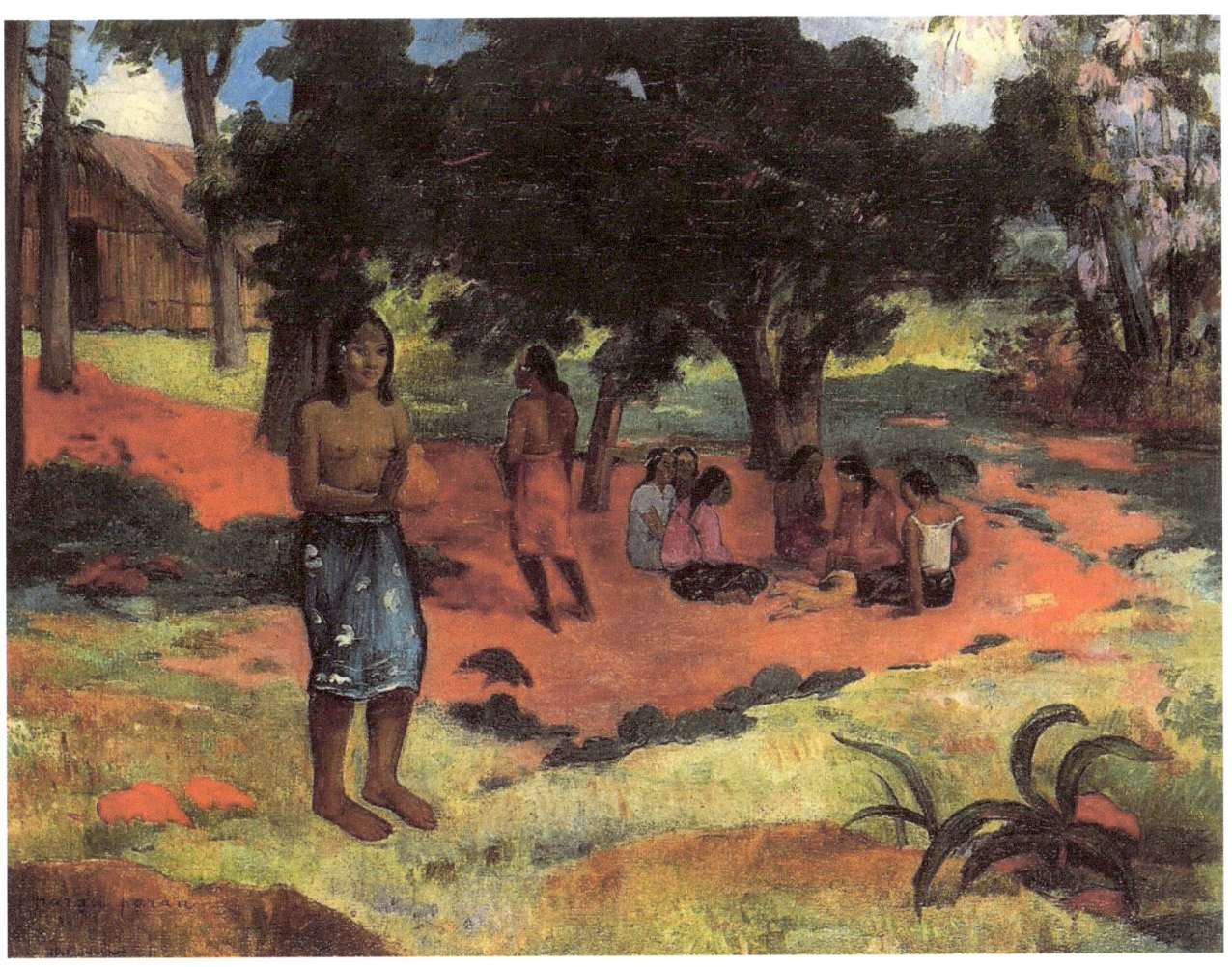

Whispered Words——1892--French Polynesia--Cloisonnism--1st Tahiti period

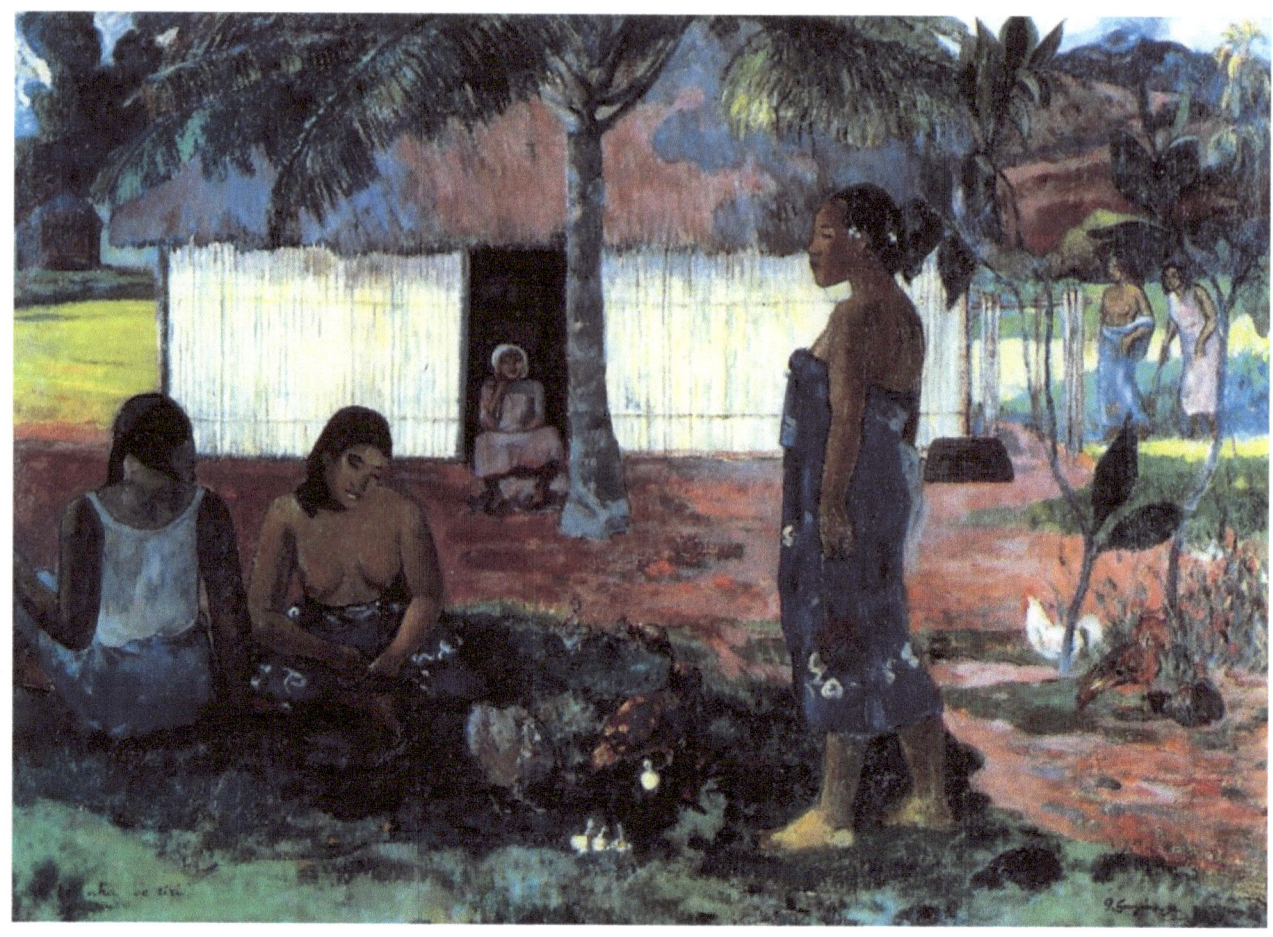

Why Are You Angry? —1896--French Polynesia--Cloisonnism--2nd Tahiti period

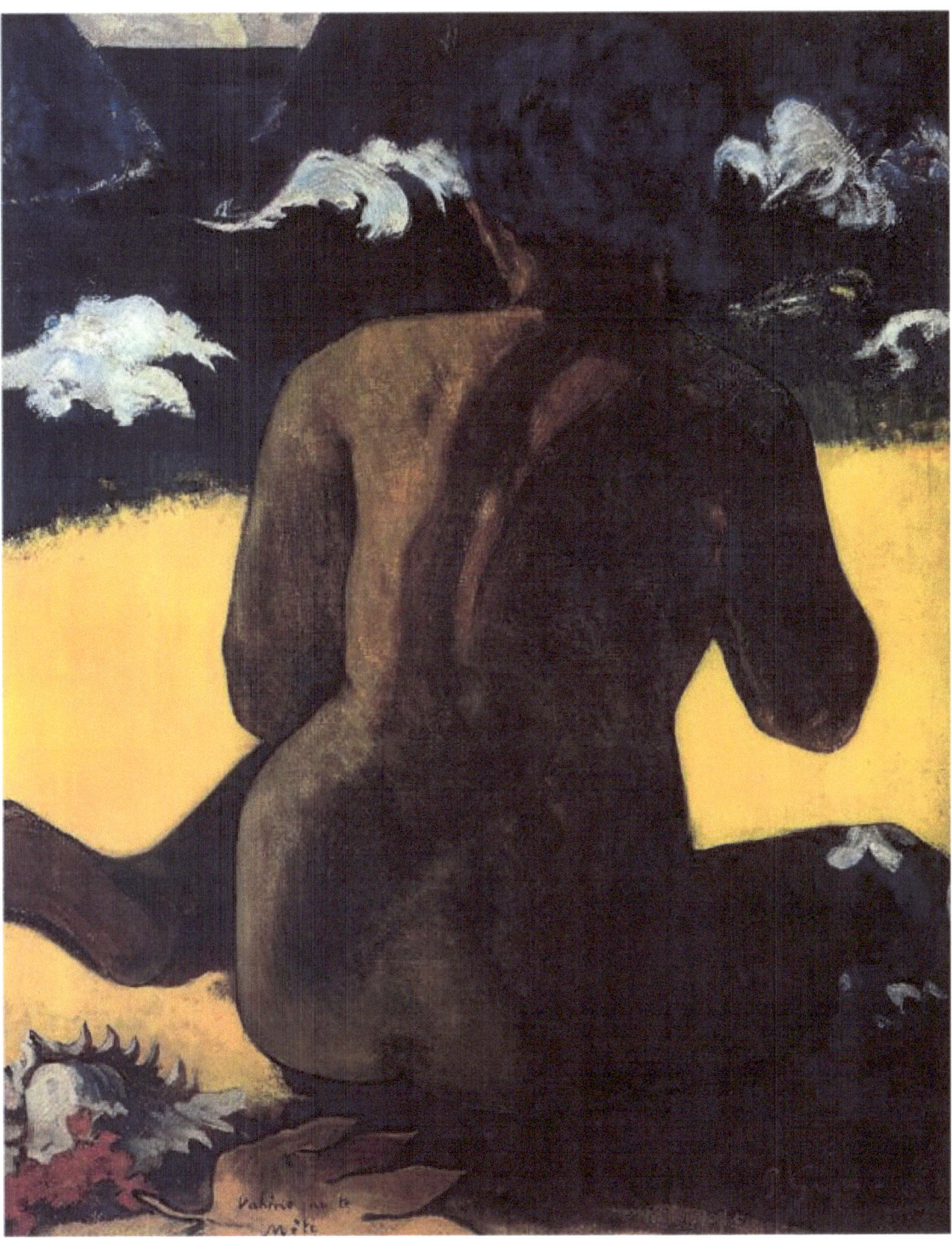

Woman by the sea——1892--French Polynesi--Cloisonnism--1st Tahiti period

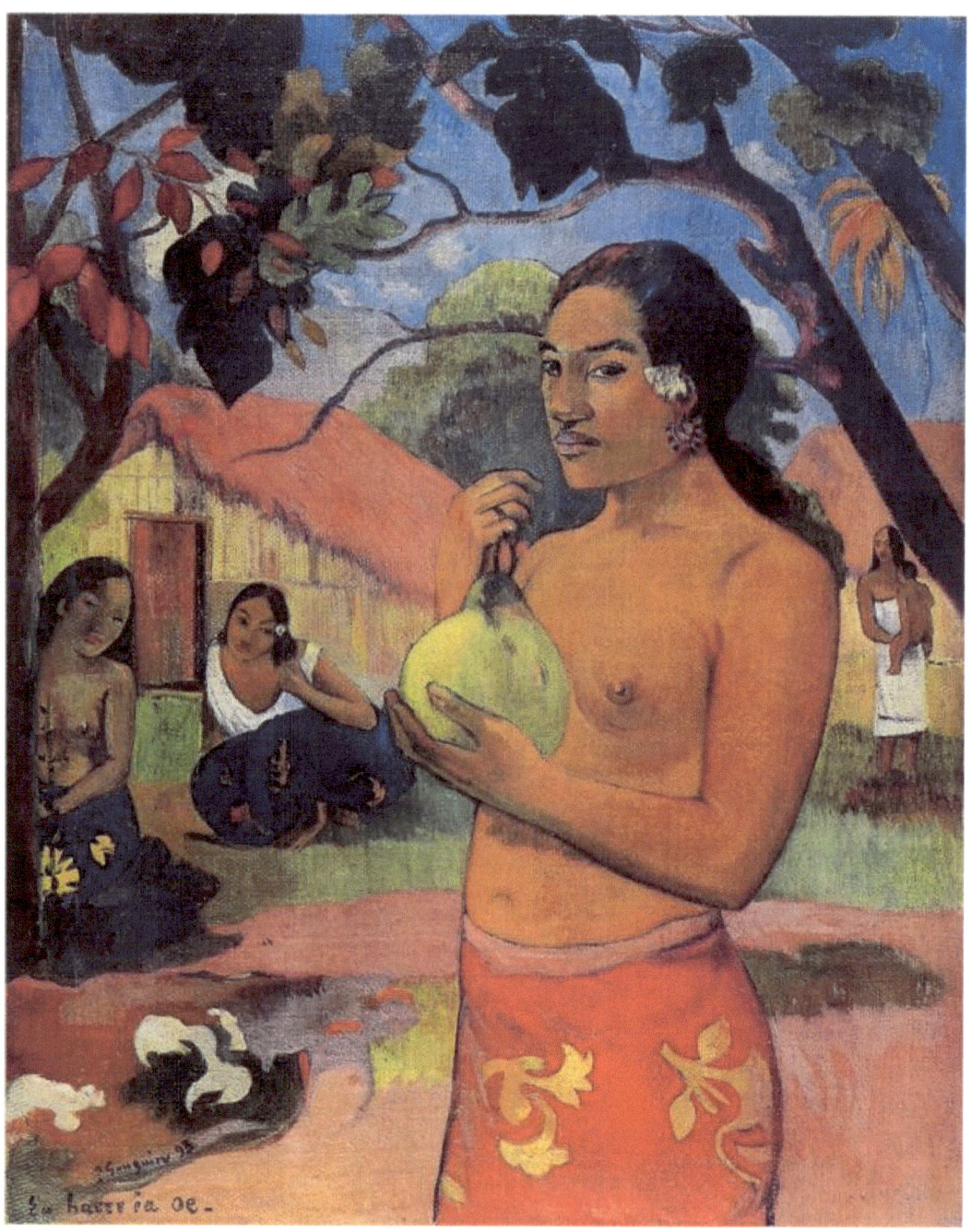

Woman Holding a Fruit——1893--French Polynesia--Post-Impressionism--
1st Tahiti period

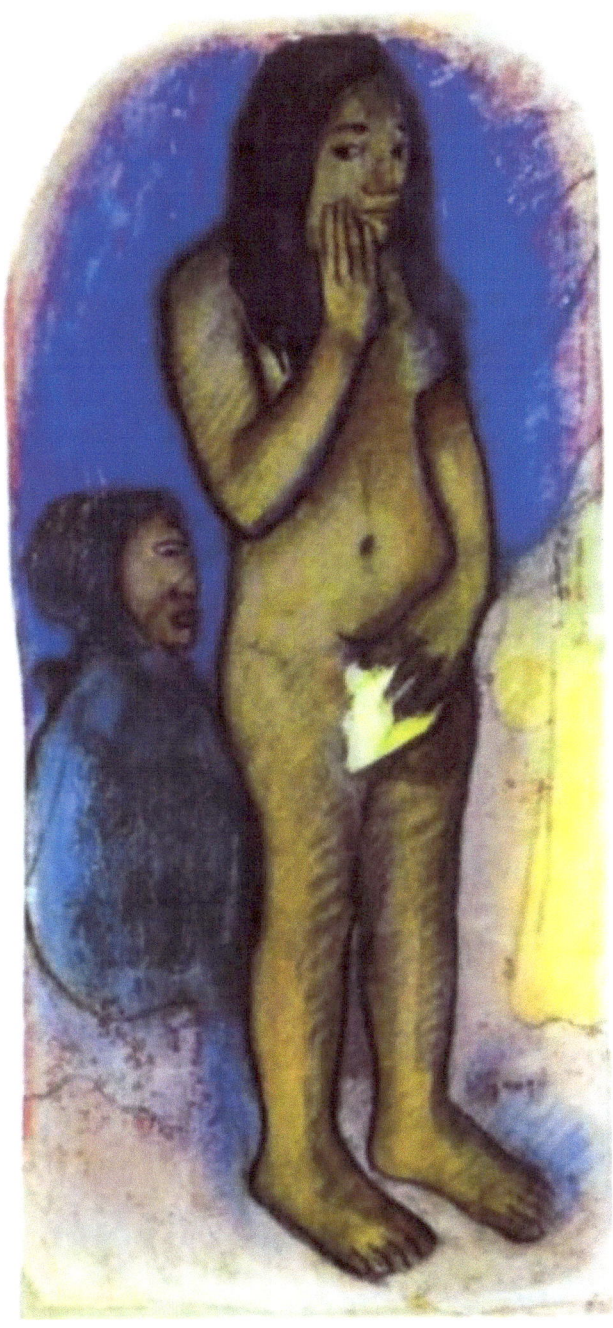

Words of the Devil──1892--French Polynesia--Post-Impressionism--1st Tahiti period

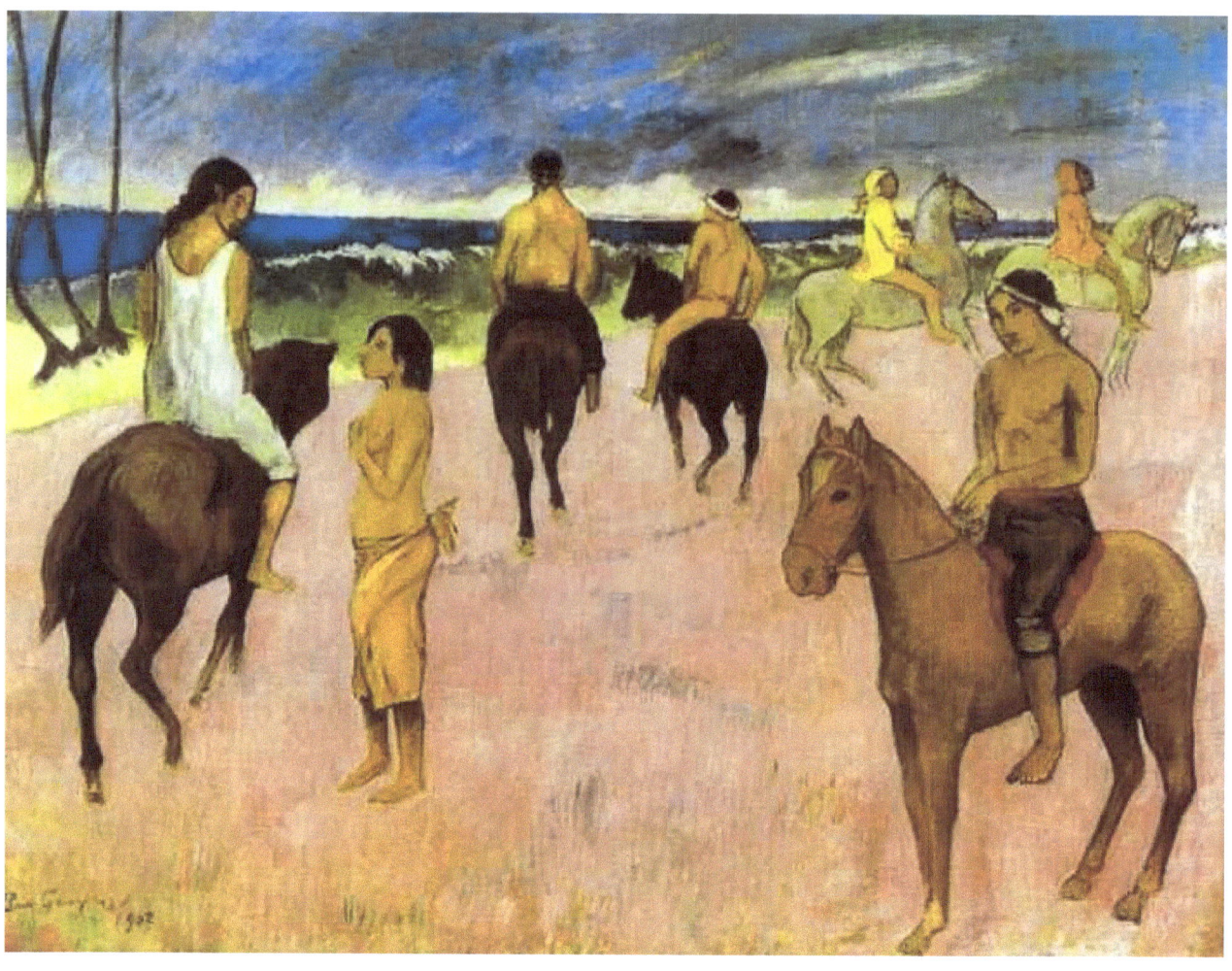

Riders on the beach II——1902--French Polynesia--Cloisonnism--2nd Tahiti period

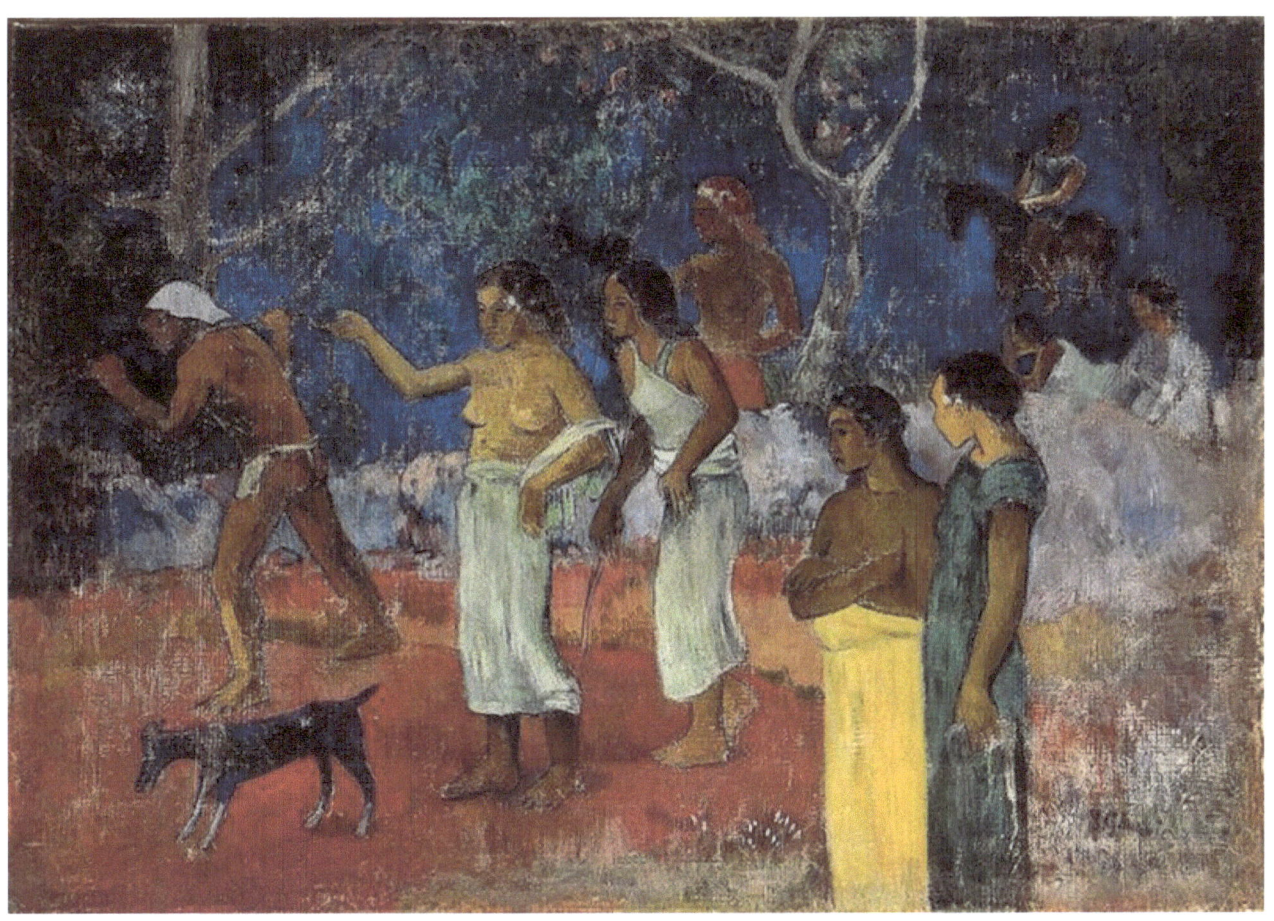

Scene from Tahitian Life——1896--Post-Impressionism--2nd Tahiti period

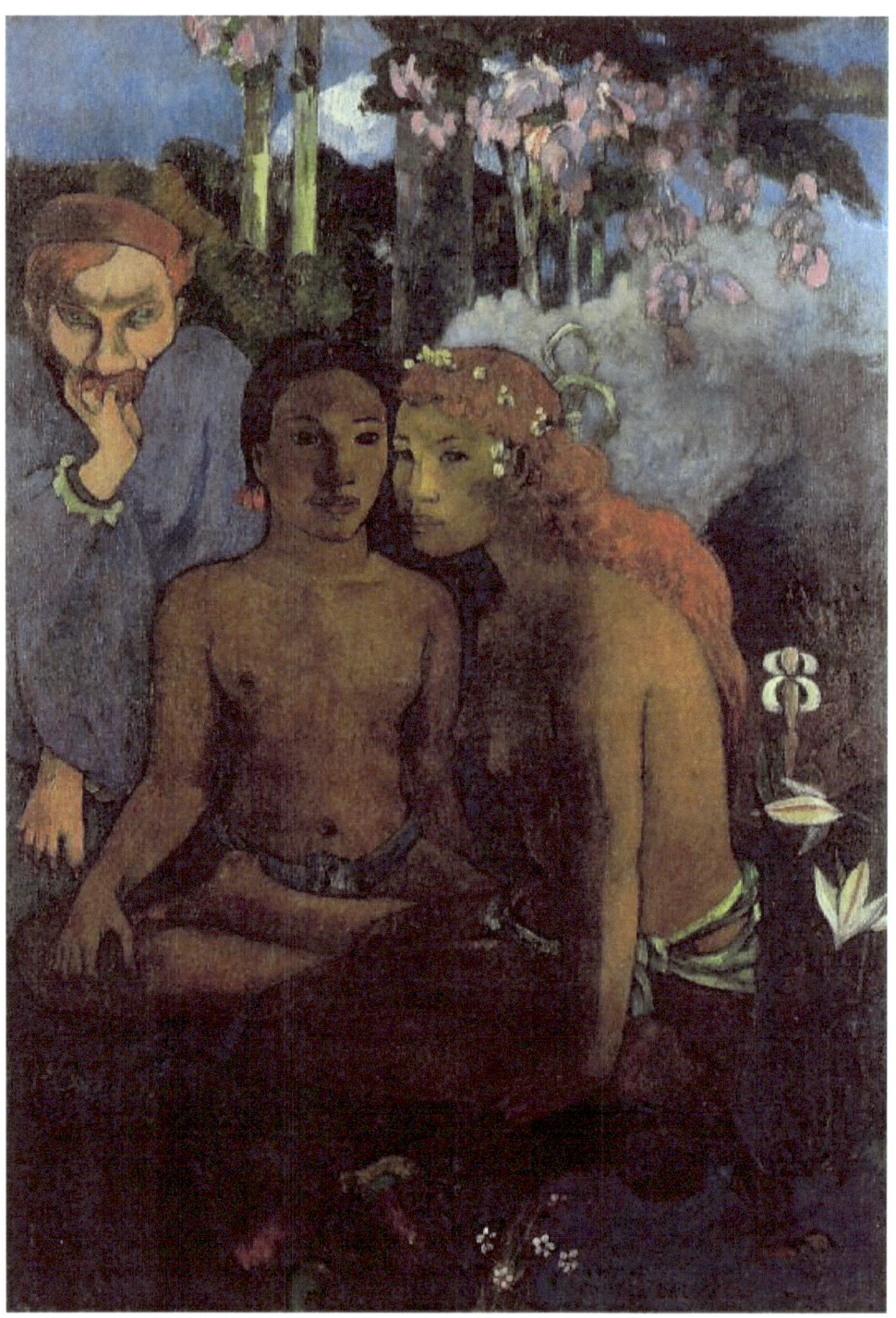

Barbarous Tales--1902--French Polynesia--Post-Impressionism--
2nd Tahiti period

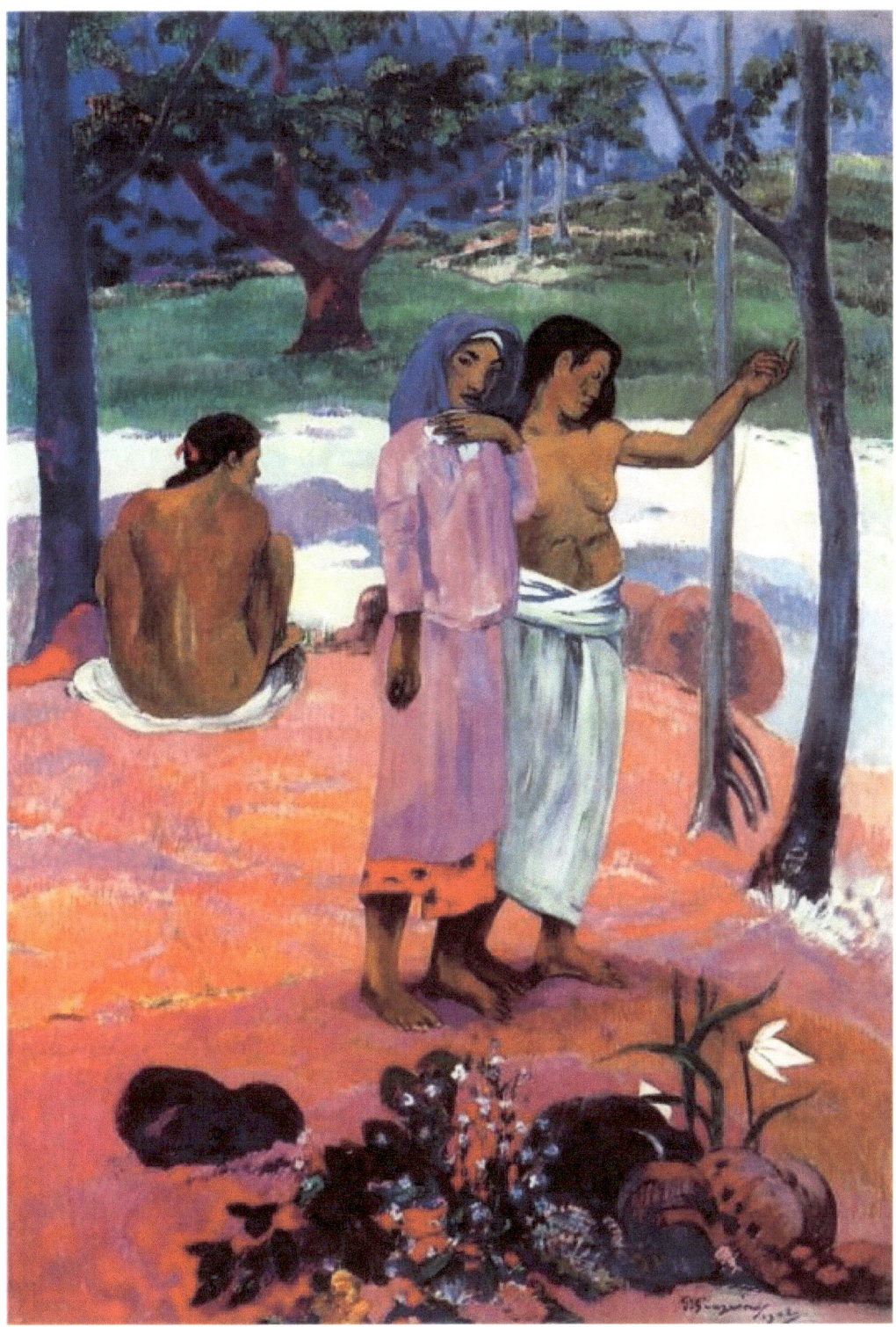

The Call—1902--French Polynesia--Cloisonnism--2nd Tahiti period

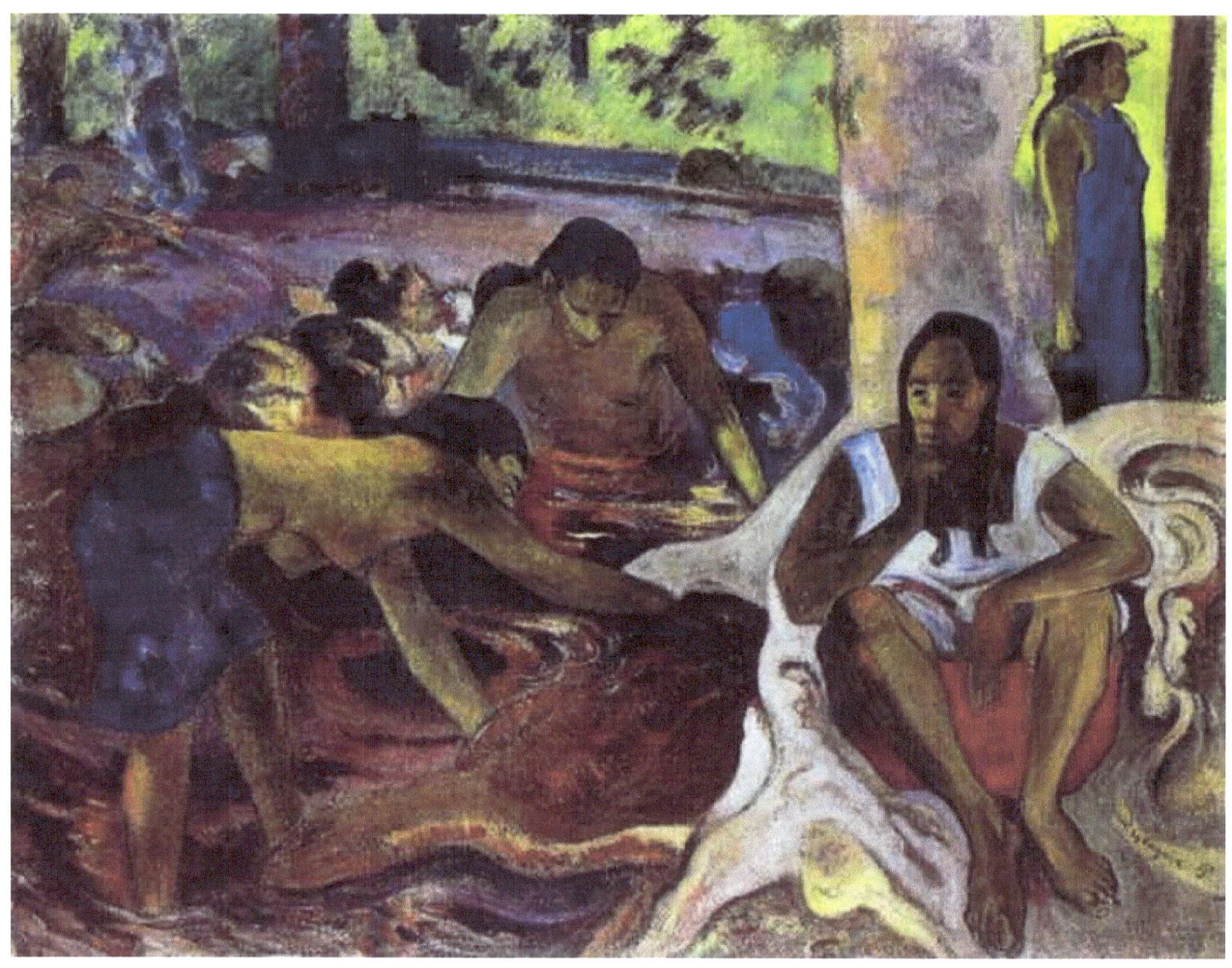

The fisherwomen of Tahit—189--French Polynesia--Cloisonnism--1st Tahiti period